Dr. Bill Thrasher's book should be placed in the hands of every new Christian. This is a splendid invitation to much more than a spiritual discipline, it is a call to an exciting way of life with our personal and loving Lord.

> LYLE W. DORSETT
> Professor of Evangelism and Spiritual Formation
> Wheaton College

Bill Thrasher is 'a man after my own heart' —one who lives and walks in prayer and fasting as a normal lifestyle, not dry religious duty. This very solid and balanced book studies how God is always desiring to orchestrate prayer-filled eruptions and expressions from the conditions of our daily life and calling— some which might appear difficult and challenging, but which often bring the most precious and delightful spiritual returns. One of the most truly refreshing studies on prayer to appear in years.

> GARY P. BERGEL
> President, Intercessors for America/Youth
> Interceding for America

Bill Thrasher's new book is a solid read for anyone who struggles to succeed in making prayer a serious and strategic part of daily life. I think you'll find *A Journey to Victorious Praying* a welcome companion on your path to prevailing prayer.

> PHIL MIGLIORATTI
> National Pastors Prayer Network

This is a valuable guidebook for the serious believer who wants to move ahead in the exciting miracle of prayer. I trust it will be read widely and be used of God to bring to our churches the prayer revival we desperately need.

WARREN W. WIERSBE
Author and conference speaker

Today more than ever we need to sharpen our prayer life, not to make it more professional, but to make it more effective. In this book, Bill Thrasher helps us understand how. Where we expect to read about courage and strength in prayer, he draws aside the curtain on our weakness and unworthiness. Where we expect to quicken our prayer pace, he counsels waiting. And where we expect to intensify our petition, he speaks of praise. You'll be glad you spent time with this excellent book.

V. GILBERT BEERS
President, Scripture Press Ministries

My good friend Bill Thrasher in his book *A Journey to Victorious Praying* takes us by the hand on this journey to effectual fervent prayer with well researched biblical instruction, personal affirmations, and powerful demonstrations of the disciplines and delights of prayer. It is my personal heart-cry that God will mightily use this handbook to develop the prayer life of every one of us. Nothing is more needed in the church today.

STEPHEN F. OLFORD
Founder of the Stephen Olford Center for
Biblical Preaching

A JOURNEY TO

Victorious Praying

FINDING

DISCIPLINE

AND DELIGHT

IN YOUR

PRAYER LIFE

Bill Thrasher

MOODY PUBLISHERS
CHICAGO

All Scripture quotations, unless otherwise indicated, are taken from the *New American Standard Bible*®, Copyright © 1960, 1962, 1963, 1968, 1971, 1972, 1973, 1975, 1977, 1995 by The Lockman Foundation. Used by permission. (www.Lockman.org)

Cover photography: © 2003 Juan Silva/The Image Bank

Library of Congress Cataloging-in-Publication Data

Thrasher, Bill, 1952-
    A journey to victorious praying: finding discipline and delight in your prayer life/Bill Thrasher.
        p.cm.
    ISBN: 0-8024-3698-6
    ISBN-13: 978-0-8024-3698-6
1. Prayer—Christianity. I. Title.
BV210.3.T47 2003
248.3´2—dc21

                                                                2003001413

We hope you enjoy this book from Moody Publishers. Our goal is to provide high-quality, thought-provoking books and products that connect truth to your real needs and challenges. For more information on other books and products written and produced from a biblical perspective, go to www.moodypublishers. com or write to:

Moody Publishers
820 N. LaSalle Boulevard
Chicago, IL 60610

5 7 9 10 8 6

Printed in the United States of America

Dedicated to the Lord,
who delights in the prayers of His people (Proverbs 15:8),
and to my wife, Penny,
my mother, Carolyn Thrasher,
and my parents-in-law, Bill and Marybelle Bauer,
who have lovingly interceded for my life and ministry

ABOUT THE AUTHOR

BILL THRASHER is a professor of Bible and Theology at the Moody Graduate School of the Moody Bible Institute in Chicago. He is a frequent speaker for churches and retreats across the country, and the author of *Living the Life God Has Planned.* Bill and his wife, Penny, have three sons.

Contents

Foreword

Seldom have I met a Christian who is satisfied with his or her prayer life. After years of walking with God, many of us still struggle with failures in the midst of our successes. We all have read stories of the great men and women of the Christian faith who have diligently sought God and achieved great results. We wish that we could be like them, but alas, we fall short.

This book is worthy of your consideration because of its simplicity and practicality. Here we learn not so much the theology of prayer as the practice of it; we are given examples of how to pray and what to do when our prayer life becomes routine, unsatisfying, and sometimes non-existent. The author gives us help despite our broken resolutions and our failed attempts to join the ranks of the mighty. There is help here for the struggling believer as well as the one who has been on the prayer journey for many years.

Best of all, this book is written by someone who practices what he preaches. Bill Thrasher believes in prayer and knows both the joys of receiving an answer and the disappointment that comes when God says no. Read these pages and you will sense his heart; he will take you by the hand and say, "Come with me and I will show you what I have learned in my own walk with the Savior."

In the end, it is not knowing about prayer that will change our lives, but rather actually doing it. My suggestion is that you read a chapter of this book every day and then apply what you have read. Your faith will grow and your confidence in God will encourage you to pray even more. If it is true that "more things are wrought by prayer than this world dreams of," this book will help you dream new dreams and see God at work.

Enjoy these pages. Read them with one question in mind: "How can I progress to the next level of intimate prayer with my heavenly Father?" This book will help you in your journey.

And now, before you read, pray and ask God to help you to grasp and apply the lessons that are even now in your hands. Your life will be different because you took the time to receive help from a fellow traveler.

Erwin Lutzer
Moody Church
Chicago

Acknowledgments

It is a pleasure to acknowledge my debt to the Lord Jesus Christ, who has graciously met me in my weakness and freed me from many misconceptions about prayer in order to teach me His refreshing truths. I am indebted to the loving and intimate prayer of my dear wife, Penny, and the companionship of my three sons, Will, Michael, and David.

I am grateful to Greg Thornton for his support in this project and for the capable team of Moody Publishers that made the idea of this book a reality. I would also acknowledge the capable editorial assistance of Cheryl Dunlop and thank Ee-Boon Tan who so carefully typed the manuscript.

I am also grateful to the wonderful colleagues and so many precious students at the Moody Bible Institute who have enriched my life. Special thanks to former and present graduate school deans—B. Wayne Hopkins and Joe Henriques—who have allowed me to teach a course on prayer at the Moody Graduate School for many years.

Introduction

During a vacation our family gathered together one morning to have a time of worship together. After reading some Scripture, I instructed the family, "Let's all go down to the Lake Michigan beach and take a thirty-minute walk. During this time I would like each of you to observe God's creation and come back with one thing for which you would like to bless and praise God. Also ask God to give you an encouraging word for each member of the family that you can share with them after the walk. Now I would like there to be no talking during this thirty-minute walk. It will be a time of silence." Everyone seemed to clearly understand and agree to my instructions.

I was the last one to walk down from the cottage to the beach, arriving about five minutes after everyone else. What I saw disturbed me. Everyone was talking loudly and feverishly scurrying about on the beach. As I was about to speak I learned that my son's retainer had fallen out of his mouth into Lake Michigan. When I thought about having to spend five hundred dollars on a replacement, I began to encourage the talking and the frantic activity.

Every inch of the location where the retainer dropped was diligently searched, to no avail. I called the family together on the beach for a time of prayer. We cried out to the Lord to do the impossible. "Lord, help us locate this retainer that is somewhere in Lake Michigan." My father-in-law offered up his prayer affirming that we could in no way find this "needle in a haystack" on this extremely windy day without the intervention of the Lord.

Every member of the family—seven of us—began to look along the beach to see where the retainer had possibly drifted. We walked up and down the beach and diligently searched for about a half-mile radius, all to no avail. Noticing that the wind was clearly blowing one way, we decided to take a two-mile walk to continue looking. At that moment one of my sons shouted, "We found it!" My mother-in-law had located it on the beach. We all gathered together and thanked the Lord for the merciful answer to prayer.

God has special answers to prayer for you and me— for there are lost things and people that He yearns to use you to find and restore, and many are far more significant than a lost retainer. My prayer is that this book will inspire you to call on the Lord in all the things that concern you, and in the process you will discover the great, holy, and kind God who answers prayer and desires to show Himself strong on your behalf.

SECTION

Help of Your Weakness

*We will be entrusted with special
difficulties that provide golden
opportunities to pray—this is what to do.*

1

Transforming
Fear into Faith

I discovered an astonishing truth:
God is attracted to weaknesses. He can't
resist those who humbly and honestly
admit how desperately they need Him.

꽃·JIM CYMBALA

In April of 1982 I heard a Christian leader tell the great
benefit of applying the principle of firstfruits to the
use of his time. As he had deliberately given to the Lord
the first few minutes of each day, the first day of the week,
and the first few days of each new year, he had experienced
special joys and blessings. I listened attentively as he spoke
and began to process the possible application of the truth
to my life. The discipline of giving to the Lord the first
moments of a day and the first day of the week were
things that I was already attempting to practice. However,
I had never thought of giving the first few days of a year
to the Lord, so I proceeded to make a note in my future
planning to seek to do that in January of 1983.

When January arrived I was very tired. However, as a

professor, I had a few days before my classes started, and I told the Lord that I desired to present those days to Him for His purposes. As I sought the Lord, He gave a few ideas of how to make use of this time. I first of all made an attempt to declutter my life and got rid of some clothes and some other possessions that had not been used in the past few years. During those days I also looked at some past journals that I had written. In this time three things stood out to me that gave me direction for the new year. I made a conscious decision to go into 1983 trusting God for those three things. The year was one of the most fruitful of my life as I had never previously deliberately entered a year trusting God that He would do specific things in my life during that year. I prayed for Him to allow me to see the beauty of His character in a new way, to be overwhelmed with His personal love for me, and to understand in a fresh way what it meant for Christ to be my life.

When the next year came around I decided to do the same thing and seek God to once again give me three things for which to trust Him for that new year. This has become a yearly practice. In 1990 one of the things that I went into the year asking God for was to be used of Him to raise up prayer among His people. As I pray these requests during the year, I try to keep notes on the answers and insight God is pleased to give. As I sought God for a year about this matter of how to be used of Him in this way, I learned only one insight. It is this insight that I would like to present in this section of the book. God showed me that the way to raise up prayer among His people was to share with them how to make use of their "needy moments."

DISCOVERING OUR NEED OF GOD

What is prayer? O. Hallesby, one of Norway's leading Christian teachers, said that prayer is an attitude of our hearts toward God. It is an attitude of helplessness. This attitude of helplessness is not meant to drive you to anxiety but rather to drive you to God. In other words, prayer is helplessness plus faith. We may stumble over this until we realize that faith is simply coming to Christ with our helplessness. When we petition God in prayer, we come to Christ and tell Him what we and those for whom we pray are lacking. It is opening up our needy lives to Him.

Let us be very specific in defining some of our "needy moments" that promote this attitude of helplessness that can give birth to true prayers. Let us look at times when we tend to be fearful and anxious.

One year I asked God to give me clear insight into my own unhealthy fears. If you do this you may be surprised how significant a motivating force fear is in your life. For example, ask the Lord, "What are things I say or do not say and things I do or do not do that are motivated by a fear of rejection?" The relevance of this is that we are to seek God in prayer at every point of our fears. Look at Psalm 34:4: "I sought the Lord, and He answered me, and delivered me from all my fears."

As we seek God at our point of fears, we need to look

for specific promises that can transform our fear responses into faith responses. The first time I was asked to speak on a nationwide radio broadcast and answer questions from people who would call in from the audience, I agreed to pray about it. My fear was what would happen if I could not answer the questions. As I sought God He used Psalm 67:7 to assure my heart and calm my fears. That verse says, "God blesses us, that all the ends of the earth may fear Him." I saw the principle that I could count on God's blessing as I sought to benefit others. God is eager to help us process our fears as we seek Him in prayer.

In Philippians 4:6 God graciously commands us to "be anxious for nothing." If He stopped there with His instruction it would only make us more anxious. Now we would be more anxious because we would also realize that we are clearly disobeying God!

In God's kindness He also instructs us how to process our anxiety. Every time you are tempted to be fearful or anxious, view it as a prompting of the Lord to pray. God uses three words to explain this process—prayer, supplication, and thanksgiving. In prayer we talk to God about our anxiety. We may even need to ask Him what it is that is bothering us. In supplication we petition Him and tell Him what we would like Him to do about it. You will never have real peace until you do. In thanksgiving you turn your attention away from the problem and to God. If you only prayed and supplicated or petitioned, and neglected thanksgiving, you would become more wrapped up in the problem. Thanksgiving links your heart to God as you praise Him for His knowledge and concern of the situation as well as His desire to carry the burden.

CASTING OUR ANXIETIES ON THE LORD

In prayer God can train us to cast our cares upon Him (1 Peter 5:7). Some anxieties are easier than others to cast upon God. The more something means to you, the harder it is to trust God with it. God tells us that when Abraham offered up Isaac on the altar, his faith was "perfected" (James 2:22). It was "perfected" in that God's *goal* for Abraham had been reached. His goal is to train His people to trust Him with the most precious thing of their lives. The most precious gift of God to Abraham was his beloved son Isaac. In previous times he had had lapses of faith where fear struck him and Abraham took matters into his own hands (Genesis 12, 20). At this time he had come to the point that he could trust God with his most precious gift—even when being asked to do something that he did not fully understand (Genesis 22; Hebrews 11:17–19).

What is your "Isaac"? Are you willing to surrender the matter to God and realize that He is able to guard what you entrust to Him (2 Timothy 1:12)? What *you* try to control is up to *you* to worry about and work out. Let this battle be used of God to raise up many times of precious prayer. Why not talk to Him right now about your "Isaac"?

Praying with Confidence When You Feel Unworthy

God is not aloof. He says continually
through the centuries, "I'll help you,
I really will. When you're ready to throw
up your hands, throw them up to Me."

&-JIM CYMBALA

A pastor told me about a personal experience that has
been a great help when I feel inadequate and unworthy of God's blessing as I pray. He said that after a very
difficult day he was trying to pray before he went to bed.
As he sought God amidst the discouragement of this difficult day, he thought to himself, *Would you have any problem
praying if you had led somebody to Christ today and had a great time
studying the Scripture?* He reflected on this thought and responded to himself, *No, I would have no problem praying; but this
is not the kind of day I had. I have had an awful day that has been characterized by many wrong responses.* During this time of seeking
God and reading the Scriptures, he related how he sensed
a loving rebuke from God as he reflected on praying in

Christ's name: "Do you want to come to Me in *your* name
or in *Jesus'* name?" Only when we learn to pray in Jesus'
name can we use our times of feeling unworthy and inadequate and turn them into confident intercession.

What is meant by the concept of "name" in Scripture? It refers to one's character. God's changing a person's
name foreshadowed a change of character that He
planned to work in that person's life (cf. John 1:42). It
also refers to one's corresponding reputation. In this sense
the Bible refers to the desirability of a "good name"
(Proverbs 22:1). Third, it may refer to one's authority. If
you made a request to a fellow employee, and he seemed
reluctant to follow through, would it not radically change
things if you informed him that the request is being en-
dorsed or authorized by the president of the company?

We are to come to God in Jesus' name (John 14:14).
We must pray for things that are in line with His revealed
character and for requests in which His answers would enhance His reputation. We are also to come to God in
Jesus' authority. I will never deserve God's blessing and
neither will you, but that is not the point. The marvelous
truth is that because of God's grace, Jesus died in order
that we could experience all of His blessings (Ephesians
1:3). We must humble ourselves before God and receive
His gracious gifts. God's name is honored as He forgives
our sin, for it shows His loving, merciful, wise, and righteous character (Psalm 25:11). His name is honored as
He gives us guidance (Psalm 23:4) and allows His people
to experience His rest (Isaiah 63:14). When a sheep ends

up in the right place, discerning people do not praise the sheep but rather the loving and caring Shepherd.

The key is to come to God with confidence during your needy moments. Humble yourself before Him and let Him use your life to display to the world how kind and gracious He is (Ephesians 2:7—look it up!). At the Tower of Babel the people arrogantly attempted to make a name for themselves (Genesis 11:4). A believer in Christ has the awesome privilege of living for God's name (Psalm 115:1). In all of life our wonderful Lord can teach us how to draw attention to Him—even in the routine of life (1 Corinthians 10:31; Colossians 3:17). This will happen as we learn to come to Him not in our own name but in Jesus' name.

Sharing Your True Desires with God

I had rather teach one man to
pray than ten men to preach.

❧D. L. MOODY

A student, I will call him Jim, told an exciting testimony of a very valuable lesson he had learned in prayer. Jim's struggle with an ungodly habit in his life led him to cry out to God for deliverance. Nothing happened. One day a person came up and had the love and discernment to graciously confront Jim by saying, "Why are you asking God to deliver you from this ungodly habit? You love this ungodly habit. You do not really want God to answer your prayer." Jim admitted that this was precisely the truth.

Jim said that one of the most humbling things he had ever done was to come to God and tell Him that he loved this ungodly habit and did not really want Him to answer his prayer for deliverance. Jim also informed me that this honest prayer was the beginning of the process of breaking him from the habit!

This testimony helped opened up the truth of Hebrews 4:16 to me. We are told to "draw near with confidence to the throne of grace." My question was, How do I come to God with confidence when I am thinking the wrong things, and I know I have the wrong attitude? The answer is knowing what He means when God says to "draw near with confidence." To "draw near with confidence" means to come with freedom to the throne of grace in the authority of Christ. This is what Jim did when he came to God and told Him that he loved the ungodly habit. How does God respond when we do this? Exactly as He has said He would—by sending His mercy and grace (Hebrews 4:16). His mercy speaks of His empathetic and understanding aid; His grace refers to His timely enablement that He gives to those who humble themselves before Him (James 4:6).

There are many opportunities throughout each day that encourage you to draw near with confidence to God's throne of grace. When you are struggling with anger, you need His merciful and gracious aid. You will receive it only if you first come to God and tell Him about your struggle. The first step is to honestly admit to the Lord, "I am struggling and am angry at _____, and I desperately need Your help." When you are angry your soul is hurting. Unrighteous anger is the wrong response to this hurt, but God is not indifferent about your pain. You can draw near with confidence to His throne of grace and ask Him to put His healing touch upon your heart. As Jesus walked the earth, His compassionate touch transformed the lives of those whom society looked upon as completely incurable. One word and one touch forever changed the impenitent leper in Mark 1:40–42. This same Jesus is our risen Lord today, and He cares about the hurts of your soul. Although He is opposed to the proud, He deeply desires to pour out His gracious help to those who come to Him in true humility. It is this grace that can heal your heart and give you assurance that He can even work together for your ultimate good the past hurts of your life that are so painful.

The conviction that God can work together for good the pain in *your* life cannot be reached without drawing near to the throne of grace. As Betty processed the pain of her life with an alcoholic and irresponsible father, she greatly struggled. The breakthrough came when she first admitted the struggle and in time began to see how God had used this experience to give her a deep sense of gratitude to her own husband for his life of sobriety. Her heart was filled with joy when he would simply come home at night from work! She had a profound gratefulness for a man who would bring home a paycheck that had not already been foolishly squandered. This grateful joy was a part of the good that God had graciously worked out of her pain. God uses the past and present difficulties of your life to lead you into a life of prayer.

No one ever just decides to be a prayer warrior. God does something in a life that makes the person sense this need of God. Theologian John Calvin called prayer "the discipline of your weakness." As you process the temptations of your life, this is another wonderful opportunity to pray. But how do you pray? One of the most liberating verses of the Bible to me is 1 John 1:7, "But if we walk in the Light as He Himself is in the Light, we have fellowship with one another, and the blood of Jesus His Son cleanses us from all sin." To walk in the light is to walk openly, honestly, and transparently before God and His truth. If you will take your temptations and turn them into conversations with God, you will learn to talk to God from your *heart*. Temptations are an appeal to meet righteous needs in an unrighteous way. Come to God; thank Him that He has a righteous way to meet the longing your temptation has stirred.

When Nathan rebuked David for his sin of adultery and murder, he reminded David of God's gracious blessings,

> *Nathan then said to David, "You are the man! Thus says the Lord God of Israel, 'It is I who anointed you king over Israel and it is I who delivered you from the hand of Saul. I also gave you your master's house and your master's wives into your care, and I gave you the house of Israel and Judah; and if that had been too little, I would have added to you many more things like these!'"* (2 Samuel 12:7–8)

Notice that He says, "if that had been too little, I would have added to you many more things like these." In other words, David was reproved for doubting God's goodness and yielding to his deceitful desires. When we fail to come to God with the thirst of our heart, we place ourselves in a very vulnerable situation. Listen as Nathan continues his rebuke:

> "Why have you despised the word of the Lord by doing evil in His
> sight? You have struck down Uriah the Hittite with the sword, have
> taken his wife to be your wife, and have killed him with the sword of
> the sons of Ammon. Now therefore, the sword shall never depart from
> your house, because you have despised Me and have taken the wife of
> Uriah the Hittite to be your wife. Thus says the Lord, 'Behold, I will
> raise up evil against you from your own household; I will even take
> your wives before your eyes and give them to your companion, and he
> will lie with your wives in broad daylight. Indeed you did it secretly,
> but I will do this thing before all Israel, and under the sun.'" Then
> David said to Nathan, "I have sinned against the Lord." And Nathan
> said to David, "The Lord also has taken away your sin; you shall not
> die. However, because by this deed you have given occasion to the ene-
> mies of the Lord to blaspheme, the child also that is born to you shall
> surely die." (2 Samuel 12:9–14)

David lived before Christ, but the Law gave him correct ways to approach God that pointed ahead to Christ's
coming and His sacrifice. In the days since the coming of
Christ, we are to come to Him and let Him quench the
thirst of our heart (John 6:35; 7:38). There can be grave
consequences for failing to draw near with confidence to
the throne of grace and let Jesus' pure provision quench
our thirst. Why not right now reach a solemn conviction
to "walk in the Light" with each temptation of your life?
Purpose to let every point of temptation lead you into a
conversation with God and trust Him to meet the deepest
thirsts of your heart.

If you have been deceived and have drunk from the
polluted wells of sin, make a clean break with this pattern

of behavior and tell someone today of your decision. As you draw near with confidence to God's throne of grace, continually depend upon His empathetic mercy and enabling grace. Let any consequence of the behavior of the past serve as a loving reminder of the need to continually walk openly, honestly, and transparently before the Lord.

Turning Your Temptations into Victorious Prayer

*God wins His greatest victories
in the midst of apparent defeat.*

D r. John Perkins is a respected Christian leader who has been used of God to graciously lead the church in racial reconciliation. The accomplishments of his life are numerous as his ministries have given hope to thousands of people. I have been deeply moved by his testimony of coming to God in humble prayer. After his conversion as an adult he yearned to understand the Bible. He struggled with great frustration in studying Scripture since he had only been privileged to go to school through the third grade. He came to God and said, "O God, open up Your Word to me and I'll be faithful to obey it and proclaim it." God heard this humble cry, and the testimonies of countless numbers of people assure us of God's abundant answer to his prayer. The man with a third-grade education has been awarded seven honorary doctorates!

Our times of great weakness may be the precursor of

special opportunities. This is one of the "ways of God." Many times great difficulties precede special works of God. You can even say that God wins His greatest victories in the midst of apparent defeat. This can be clearly demonstrated in the life of our Lord on earth. When Jesus was crucified and placed in the tomb, it looked like the forces of unrighteousness had triumphed. However, it was in this time of apparent defeat that our victory for our salvation was won. This time of apparent defeat was followed by the resurrection of Christ.

In the future, unnamed godly witnesses will be used of God in a special way according to Revelation 11. They will be given special protection by God and the ability to do miracles (vv. 4–6). The future world leader known as the Antichrist will kill these godly individuals, and the enemies of righteousness will even deny them the dignity of a proper burial. Using the humiliation of these two witnesses as an occasion to rejoice, the world will have a special celebration in which gifts will be exchanged (vv. 7–10). It is at this time that the Lord will suddenly intervene and restore life to these martyrs, and their enemies will witness their being called up to heaven. Then He will send an earthquake, and seven thousand people will be killed. Those who survive the earthquake will fear and glorify the God of heaven. Once again God will win His victory in the midst of apparent defeat.

God uses the needy moments in life to prepare us for His work. Our wedding day is a very joyous memory for my wife and me. God graciously manifested His presence on that day and used the ceremony to encourage others. A Christian ministry has used the videotape of the wedding on several occasions to teach some key truths for those preparing for marriage. However, our engagement was one of the greatest spiritual battles of our lives as we learned to relate to each other as true servants without any selfish expectations. These battles that brought us low prepared us for a wonderful wedding day. The Lord used our family and friends in a very effective way.

God gave me special joy and grace in the passing of a series of written and oral exams for my doctorate. This victory in my life was preceded by a time of sickness that temporarily made it impossible to study. On my sickbed, I was reminded that God is the source of everything. The Lord allows circumstances in our life that wean us away from trusting in our ability in order to truly trust in Him (2 Corinthians 1:8–9).

A pastor on the West Coast was leading a number of people to Christ from some difficult backgrounds. He warned them that they would be tempted to go back to some of their previous immoral choices. With this spiritual danger in mind, he prepared them with a very practical strategy of what to do. He instructed, "I want you to think ahead and ask God to give a prayer burden to pray each time you are tempted to go back to your previous lifestyles. I want it to be a prayer that will damage Satan's kingdom as God answers it."

The insight is not any more complicated than he has stated it. It has been enormously helpful to me, and I have attempted to pass it on to hundreds of people. The idea is to use the temptation to do wrong as a motivation to pray. You can apply this to any persistent temptation in your own life. What if every time you are tempted to think an impure thought, you pray for the purity of your children? What if every time you are tempted to be discouraged or fearful, you prayed for God to fill your spiritual leaders with His Spirit!

The key is to ask God what He wants you to pray. It should be the prayer burden that *He* gives you. As you turn your temptation into meaningful intercession you will find yourself engaging in true prayer. If you and I had devised prayer, we would have probably designed it so that we could pray from our pride. A spirit of pride looks down on others and does not identify with their needs (Luke 18:9–12). A spirit of humility realizes one's own weakness, and God's merciful compassion flows to the person and through him to others (Luke 18:13–14). Temptation enables you to feel the needs of others and be prompted to intercede for them. In Psalm 27:8 David says, "When You said, 'Seek My face,' my heart said to You, 'Your face, O Lord, I shall seek!'" Realize that in your persistent temptation God is calling you to seek Him and turn these temptations into conversation with Him and intercession for others. Let God give you His prayer burdens for you, and let your temptations be the reminders to pray for them.

Author Wesley Duewel relates the prayer burden that God laid on Dorothy Clapp, who was an older Christian lady in New Jersey.

God led her to take as her prayer assignment a public high school down the street. Day after day, month after month, year after year she faithfully obeyed her prayer task. She prayed for God to save young people in that school. Then she began to pray that God would not only save them but send them to the ends of the earth. After twelve years of faithful praying, she began praying for a mischievous young male student. She sent him a Gospel of John. For three more years she prayed, and at last God saved George Verwer.

Before long George had led two hundred other students to Jesus Christ. Some of them went to college and began to meet daily for prayer and went out together in evangelism. In 1957, three of them went to Mexico to evangelize during their summer vacation. By 1960, they were also taking Christian youth to Spain. By 1962, they had their first multi-nation European campaign. By 1964, I had the joy of greeting George and the first Operation Mobilization group to India.

Now each year several thousand Christian young people from many nations join forces to evangelize, sell and distribute literature, and reach the nations for Christ. Operation Mobilization is reaching coastal ports by two gospel ships, training hundreds of youth each summer, and enlisting others in one- to two-year short-term service. Its "graduates" are strengthening the ranks of many Christian churches and organizations around the world.

It can be all traced to one Christian lady who prayed for fifteen years for students at a high school. Only God has the total results recorded of her faithful obedience in prayer. In heaven, she is already rejoicing. But the full record will be tallied and her full reward will be given only at the judgment throne of Christ. There, before His assembled millions of saints, Jesus will call her forward, praise her for her faithfulness, and announce her great reward.[1]

Would you lift up your heart to God and ask Him to give you His prayer burden? You might have a deep regret of a past sin. Do you realize that God is even able to heal the hurts that you have caused? Look at how Abraham's intercession was used by God to correct the harm he had caused others through his act of disobedience (Genesis 20:17–18). God is a great God. Never underestimate His power and grace to set you back on course. Let your temptations to sin draw you to the Lord! Only eternity will be able to reveal the awesome effect of your decision to use the needy moments of your life as an occasion for true prayer.

The Help of the Holy Spirit

You have a personal helper who is eager to assist you—this is how He works.

Experiencing the Spirit's Motivation in Prayer

There is nothing that makes us love
someone so much as praying for them.

❧ WILLIAM LAW

My mother is a very disciplined lady and a prayer warrior. I owe a great debt to her in the way her example has influenced my life, and I could never thank God enough for giving her to me as a mother. I also owe a lot to a college roommate who modeled before my impressionable life the discipline of prayer. I reasoned, *If Buster prays each day, I guess that is what a Christian is supposed to do.* So I sought to practice this discipline of prayer.

As I grew in the Christian life I became acquainted with more and more prayer requests. I actually tried to pray for them all until after several years my prayer life reached a tragic low. The discipline of prayer had become a big burden and I told the Lord that I felt one of the greatest gifts He could give to me was to get this burden off my back.

My prayer life had died. How do you know when your prayer life has died? When you pray with no expectancy, it has died! If you pray and do not expect anything to happen, you have to ask the honest question, "Why pray?"

Most of the teaching about prayer is that it is important and you ought to do it. I accepted both of these ideas, but there is more to prayer than the truth of its importance and the need to do it. To be sure, all teaching on prayer needs to be built upon this foundation, for without it any other insights could only be theoretical. However, I desperately needed to learn some new lessons. In this section I will attempt to share the scriptural truth that resurrected my prayer life.

God gives us a gracious instruction in Ephesians 6:18 and in Jude 20 to pray in the Holy Spirit. There are only four other direct commands in relationship to the Holy Spirit in the Bible:

Walk by the Spirit (Galatians 5:16).
Be filled with the Spirit (Ephesians 5:18).
Do not grieve the Spirit (Ephesians 4:30).
Do not quench the Spirit (I Thessalonians 5:19).

Let us take some time to examine what is included in praying in the Holy Spirit.

Jesus called the Holy Spirit a "Paraclete," which is translated "Helper" in some translations (John 14:16, 26). The meaning of the Greek word is "one who is called alongside to help." To pray in the Holy Spirit simply means to lean upon His divine help as we pray. How does He help?

John Hyde was a missionary to India who was known as "Praying Hyde." He held prayer conventions. At the end of one such convention, a dear believer was crying to God to give him a heart of love for other people, and at the same time was bemoaning his own cold and hardened heart. He was interrupted by a friend who lovingly rebuked him. He said, "Why are you looking down at your poor self, brother? Of course your heart is cold and dead. But you have asked for the broken heart of Jesus, His tears. Is He a liar? Has He not given what you asked for? Then why look down away from His heart to your own?"[1]

In other words the dear child of God needed to learn that praying in the Holy Spirit is learning to depend on the Holy Spirit to motivate us in prayer. The fruit of the Spirit is love (Galatians 5:22). Martin Luther cautioned us that prayer is not a performance but climbing up to the heart of God. It is the Holy Spirit who experientially makes this a reality in a believer's life. We will make progress when we first come to God and confess that in our own strength we are indifferent, critical, and apathetic. We need to trust the Spirit of God to produce in us a Christlike fervency and compassion. God's indictment of His people in Isaiah 64:7 was that there was no one who called on His name and aroused himself to take hold of Him in prayer. Such fervent prayer was found in Christ's prayer in Gethsemane (Luke 22:44) and in the early church as it met after Peter had been imprisoned (Acts

12:5). The love of the Spirit produces this type of fervent striving and agonizing in prayer (Romans 15:30).

How do we cooperate with the Holy Spirit to develop this type of fervency and compassion in our prayers? The first step is to respond in the Spirit as He reveals a need in your life or in another's life. The second step is to acknowledge your inability to meet this need apart from God (John 15:5). We must realize that we cannot change our own heart or the heart of another person. The third step is to let this become your continual attitude. The key to this becoming a continual attitude is to depend on the Spirit to renew it at each point of sin as we confess it and at each time of spiritual responsibility. We cannot work this up on our own strength. True spiritual fervency and compassion is a work of the Holy Spirit. As all of life is to be lived in dependence on the Holy Spirit, so in our prayer life we are to depend on the Spirit of God for our motivation.

When you have a prayer burden that reflects a deep personal concern, it is essential to be sensitive to the Holy Spirit's motivation and direction. Imagine that you had started a church and invested considerable love, time, and energy in its development. How would you respond to the members if you later learned that the church was characterized by strife, lawsuits against each other, incestual immorality, abuse of the Lord's Supper, and misuse of their spiritual gifts? Would you begin your correspondence to them by telling them you continually thank God for them? That is precisely how the Holy Spirit led Paul in his correspondence to the church at Corinth (1 Corinthians 1:4).

John Hyde had a heavy burden for a pastor in India. He began to pray for him and with great concern began to tell God how cold and indifferent this pastor was and how he was a great hindrance to God's work. While John prayed, God convicted him for his critical spirit and cooperating with the "accuser of the brethren"[2] and not with the Holy Spirit. As he was meditating on Philippians 4:8 he learned that he needed to dwell not only on things that were true, but also lovely and even worthy of praise. As he meditated upon the *truth* of the pastor's indifference, he was led astray in his praying. However, the command of Philippians 4:8 to dwell on things that are true *and* lovely *and* worthy of praise guided his thoughts in a new direction. "Is there anything I can praise You for in this pastor's life?" John asked God. He was reminded of many things that he could genuinely praise God for in the pastor's life. What was the result? He later learned that the pastor's heart had experienced revival at the exact time of his praise. Commit your concern to the Spirit of God and let Him motivate and guide you as you take it to the Lord in prayer. His motivating love is radically different than the critical spirit generated by the "accuser of the brethren."

6

Receiving Strength to Believe God

I despaired at the thought that my life
might slip away without seeing God
show Himself mightily on our behalf.

❧ JIM CYMBALA

God gave us His Spirit not only to motivate our prayers but also to empower them. It is the Spirit of God who also empowers us to submit to Jesus (Ephesians 3:16–17), to resist Satan (James 4:7), and to persevere (Romans 15:5). However, we could sum up all of His work by saying that the Spirit empowers us to believe God.

Faith is a prime target in the spiritual battle in every believer's life. Notice that Paul's concern for the Thessalonian church in regard to the tempter's work was their *faith* (1 Thessalonians 3:5). We are told to "be strong in the Lord and in the strength of His might" (Ephesians 6:10). One day in asking the Lord God what this meant, I looked up each New Testament reference that uses the Greek word translated "be strong." One reference that struck me was Romans 4:20, which stated that Abraham "grew strong in faith." The phrase "grew strong in faith" carries the meaning of "being strengthened to believe."

In prayer we are to come to God and ask Him what He desires us to believe Him for. John R. Rice used to say that prayer is not to be compared to a lovely sedan that goes sight-seeing, but rather to a truck that goes straight to the warehouse, backs up, loads, and comes home with the goods. Although this matter of believing God will be explored later, the following unusual story tells how the Spirit of God gave a young college student the conviction to believe Him in a very specific way.

Dr. Richard Harvey is one of the founders at Youth for Christ. He also served as a pastor, an evangelist, and a denominational leader. During his senior year in college he observed an unusual answer to prayer that inspired him to courageously believe God on many future occasions in his life.

The largest and most popular course at the college that Richard Harvey attended was a first-year chemistry class. Dr. Lee, the most renowned professor in the school, taught the class, and every year before Thanksgiving he lectured against prayer. He would conclude the lecture by offering a challenge to anyone who still believed in prayer. Richard Harvey recalls the occasion when he writes:

> Then [Dr. Lee] would challenge, "Is there anybody here who still believes in prayer?" And he would say, "Before you answer, let me tell you what I am going to do and what I am going to ask you to do. I will turn around,

take a glass flask and hold it at arm's length." Then he would continue, "If you believe that God answers prayer, I want you to stand and pray that when I drop this flask, it won't break. I want you to know that your prayers and the prayers of your parents and Sunday school teachers and even the prayers of your own pastors cannot prevent this flask from breaking. If you wish to have them here, we will put this off until you return after the Thanksgiving recess."[1]

No one had ever stood up to Dr. Lee's challenge until a Christian freshman learned about it. He sensed that God had given him the conviction to stand up to Dr. Lee. Finally the day came when the annual challenge would be made. Dr. Lee made it in the same way that he had done for the past twelve years. The only difference was that this time this courageous freshman responded when asked if there was somebody who still believed in prayer. Harvey recalls the events that followed:

"Well," said the professor, "this is most interesting. Now we will be most reverent while this young man prays." Then he turned to the young man, "Now you may pray."

The young man just lifted his countenance toward heaven and prayed, "God, I know that You can hear me. Please honor the name of your Son, Jesus Christ, and honor me, Your servant. Don't let the flask break. Amen."

Dr. Lee stretched his arm out as far as he could, opened his hand and let the flask fall. It fell in an arc, hit the toe of Dr. Lee's shoe, rolled over and did not break.

There was no movement of air and there were no open windows. The class whistled, clapped and shouted. And Dr. Lee ceased his annual lectures against prayer.[2]

God's Spirit gave this young freshman the conviction to believe God. Although it is not the norm to believe God that a glass flask can be dropped and not break on a concrete floor, this freshman was given the faith of a David to stand up to a Goliath. God's honor was at stake, and He graciously worked through the faith of the pure-hearted freshman.

What does the Lord desire you to believe Him for today? Depend on the Spirit to strengthen you to believe Him as you seek Him.

7

Being Guided
in Prayer

Lord, all my desire is before You; and
my sighing is not hidden from You.

—PSALM 38:9

Praying in the Spirit is leaning upon the Spirit not only
for His motivation and His enablement but also for
His guidance. Wesley Duewel was on a trip from India to
the United States and fighting a fever. He thought, *If only I
could find one Christian and ask him to pray for me.* In describing
the experience, he states, "Suddenly I felt as if a human
hand with a cool wet washcloth had wiped my brow. In-
stantly my fever, headache, nausea, and sore throat were
gone and I felt completely well. I thought, 'Who prayed
for me?'"[1] Later Duewel received a letter from a Christian
half a world away who had felt a heavy burden of prayer at
that exact time and day!

A lady named Dianne repeated a childhood story
from when her parents were missionaries in Jordan. An
angry mob marched toward the mission compound with
murderous resolution. Although the compound was

walled on all four sides, that day the gate opened. Dianne and her younger brother were playing in the courtyard as the mob advanced. She remembers a dazed look coming over the forces of the mob, who inexplicably veered left, marched to the side wall, and scrambled back over it like a stream of fire ants.

Weeks later they received a letter from her grandmother in Chicago who had been awakened in the night to pray for her family in Jordan. Gripped by a sense of impending danger, she got on her knees and began to earnestly intercede until the burden lifted. Her letter inquired what crisis the family had faced. The date and time of the letter precisely matched the date and time of the threatening mob.[2]

THE HOLY SPIRIT'S KNOWLEDGE
OF OUR HEARTS

True prayer starts with God and the prayer burden He places on our heart. For that reason the greatest discipline in prayer is the discipline of communicating with the Holy Spirit as He aids us in sharing our real concerns, burdens, and desires. I have written about how to use the Lord's day to aid this process.

God is seeking to reveal Himself to you as you seek His will. Let me offer a simple suggestion that I have found to be very helpful. This idea came to me when I set aside a special time to seek the Lord concerning the dryness in my Sunday worship experience. I had ceased to have a sense of anticipation in regard to the Lord's day. It had dwindled to a mere duty.

As I sought the Lord concerning this situation, I walked away from that day with a solemn personal conviction. The conviction was to never have a Lord's day in which I would not seek to share my heart with God. This requires preparation and the enablement of God. I take time during the week to write down the three greatest concerns of my heart, finalizing it on Saturday night. Then, going into the Lord's day, I lift up these concerns to Him. It may be an upcoming responsibility, an area in which I need direction, a relationship that needs His gracious aid, or a temptation. I write down any insight that God gives in response to the request, and I review it the next week. These sheets of paper are filed away and would be worthless to anybody else. But to me, they are a reminder that my God is a living God who knows my name and address and is willing to be involved in the affairs of my life. God reveals Himself.[3]

In prayer I used to ignore my fear or anxiety and seek to continue in my previously determined plan as I sought God. I discovered that at this point of my not paying attention to my heart, true prayer died even though I continued to be involved in the mechanics of it. When our hearts cease to pray, we are not praying. The Holy Spirit has been given to help us stay in touch with our hearts so that we may fellowship with God in a genuine way.

THE HOLY SPIRIT'S LEADING IN PRAYER

It is possible to even get bogged down in the discipline of prayer by attempting to pray through all the various requests that people give. It was a great breakthrough to realize that God was not necessarily leading me to pray for everything with equal intensity. To try to do so will kill a prayer life. To learn to let God set the agenda of our prayer life will resurrect it. "Trust in Him at all times, O people; pour out your heart before Him; God is a refuge for us" (Psalm 62:8).

God will not give any of us every prayer burden. Our responsibility is to present our lives to Him and let Him place on our hearts the prayer burden He has for us. One routine Saturday morning I arose to have some time with the Lord. I was quite ready to go about my errands for the day, but I had a great uneasiness in my spirit. Attempting to be sensitive to what I had ignored too much of my life, I sat silently before the Lord and asked Him if there was anything else about which He desired me to talk to Him. A couple of things came to mind, and then there was the thought of "safety." After I prayed for God to keep me safe that day, I felt a liberty in my spirit to go into the day. Four hours later as I was driving, another car pushed me into the lane of oncoming traffic. Somehow I avoided contact with the cars on either side of me, and all I could think was "safety." I praised God for how He had prepared me for this in prayer and confessed to Him the many times I had ignored Him by living in a spirit of rush. God knows how to prepare us for all that is ahead as we seek to be attentive to Him.

On another occasion I was taking a walk with my wife and we both had a sense of the need to pray for a neighbor boy whom we deeply love. Jeff has been a big brother to my three boys, and we love him as if he were our own son. We poured out our hearts for him in prayer as we walked. God knew that that night Jeff would be rushed to the hospital with an injury to his eye, and I would have the privilege of sitting with his parents as we trusted God to deal with the situation. Praise God all went well, and God once again showed me that He can intervene in our agenda and give us a prayer burden to prepare us for what is ahead.

I do not want to give you the impression that this happens every time I pray, for it certainly does not. However, it is necessary to be open to it. Many times I have taken walks and asked the Lord to bring to my mind anything for which He would have me pray.

As we seek to obey the Spirit's guidance in prayer, let me tell you what will often happen—*nothing!* But sometimes "nothing" means that the Spirit desires to slow us down and lead us into silence. Our society is addicted to noise, and for that reason we are often insensitive to the Spirit of God.

One day years ago my car radio broke. As I was planning to get it fixed, I sensed a restraint from the Spirit. Every time I sat in my car I turned on the radio. This is not necessarily wrong, but what was wrong was that I did not include the Lord in this decision. I needed to learn how to welcome times of silence and be more available to the Lord in letting Him bring things to my mind for which to pray. It was a wonderful year that I lived without a car radio.

The Spirit of God desires to guide you in praying your heart. The apostle Paul says, "Brethren, my heart's desire and my prayer to God for them is for their salvation" (Romans 10:1). Note the link between the desire of the heart and prayer. As you delight in God and allow Him to put His desires in your heart, you will learn true prayer. Ask God to deliver you from anything that is hindering you from praying your heart to God. What is on your heart at this moment? Ask Him to help you pray your heart's desire to Him. Say with the psalmist, "Lord, all my desire is before You, and my sighing is not hidden from You" (Psalm 38:9).

8

Receiving Help
When You Don't
Know How to Pray

God's will is exactly what you would
desire if you knew all the facts.

Ming came to me one day in great discouragement as
he told me about his ministry. He was in his late
fifties and had left his career in chemical engineering to
study for the ministry. While interning at a local church,
he visited a lady in the hospital who was very sick and also
very bitter. She informed him in no uncertain terms that
she did not desire a visit from him or anybody else from
the church. Ming responded and asked her, "Could I
please pray for you?" She reluctantly said, "OK, if you
want to." Ming related to me that as he attempted to pray
all he could do was cry. His tears were the only prayer that
he could muster.

Ming was reporting this as if it were a failure. He ob-
viously wanted some reassurance. He was probably think-
ing, *I left my career, I'm fifty years old, I'm studying for a Masters in
Bible, and all I could do was cry when I tried to pray for this lady.*

What we later learned is that the lady opened her heart to Ming and the Lord. God began to deal with her bitterness, and her health dramatically improved.

Romans 8:26–27 teaches us a valuable lesson in prayer.

> In the same way the Spirit also helps our weakness; for we do not know how to pray as we should, but the Spirit Himself intercedes for us with groanings too deep for words; and He who searches the hearts knows what the mind of the Spirit is, because He intercedes for the saints according to the will of God.

As we lean upon the Spirit's help to give us motivation, enablement, and guidance, there will sometimes be times of special weakness. This weakness is clearly defined in Romans 8:26, "for we do not know how to pray as we should." In these cases the Holy Spirit lends us a helping hand. The word *help* in Romans 8:26 is the same one used in Luke 10:40, which refers to Martha desiring Mary to "help" her. The Holy Spirit helps us in praying the deep desires of our heart to the Father, who graciously answers them.

What is the worst thing we can do when we sense this weakness of not knowing how to pray as we should? It is to pretend we know how to pray. Ming was one of the greatest men of prayer I have ever known. In his flesh he could have professionalized the moment and uttered a prayer for the ill lady. However, in the integrity of his heart he leaned upon the Spirit, and in his weakness the

Spirit of God poured out tears of compassion. Such integrity of heart was used to deliver a bitter woman. As someone has wisely said, "And when thou prayest, let thy heart be without words, rather than thy words without heart."

Augustine was a well-known leader in the early church. Before he was converted he lived a very sensual lifestyle. His plans to go to Rome prompted serious intercession from his godly mother. She prayed, "O Lord, do not let him go to Rome because he will only get into further debauchery." God did let him go to Rome. But it was in Rome that he was converted. The Spirit of God pled the deep desire of the mother for his spiritual well-being, and God answered her heart.

If we do not understand this principle it is very easy to get bitter. Sometimes when we pour out our desires to God, He *appears* to be indifferent. When the apostle Paul earnestly petitioned God for the removal of his thorn in the flesh, the request was not granted. However, in not giving this desire of Paul's heart, God gave him his deeper desire. Certainly Paul's greatest desire was to know God's grace and power in order to be the most useful servant he could possibly be. God withheld the request in order to give Paul his deepest desire and thus glorify Himself (2 Corinthians 12:7–10).

As I was sharing these truths with a group of pastors one day, a pastor spontaneously arose to his feet. He announced that he would like to tell an event from his hall of shame. He said, "One day I was running around the table and chasing and yelling at my fourteen-year-old son." In tears he reported the response of his seven-year-old Down's syndrome son by stating, "Although my seven-year-old had never previously prayed, his stuttering voice blurted out to the family, 'Hold hands, Lord please help Daddy!'"

The Holy Spirit is our gracious Helper in prayer. We need His assistance in all our prayers. We are to look to Him for our motivation, to empower us to believe God, and to guide our prayers. Sometimes we must submit to our weakness and in humility let Him pray our hearts to God. What deep desire is the Spirit pleading to God for you? Is there some longing in your heart that is seemingly not being answered? Could it be that it is because God is desiring to grant you an even deeper longing and desire of your heart?

SECTION

The Help of Companionship

*Your friends may hold the keys that unlock the
untapped potential of a powerful prayer life
—this is how they can help.*

9

Receiving Help in
Prayer from Others

We are surrounded by relationships, but driven by
accomplishment. God is the opposite. Though surrounded
by His accomplishments, He has given Himself in
relationship. Though not in need of interaction, He has
chosen to pursue it. For God fellowship is the goal.

❧ VICTORIA BROOKS

Peter was a delightful student from Edinburgh, Scot-
land, whom God sent to study at Moody Bible Institute in 1981. He also became a dear friend. After he
completed his studies at Moody, he went on to graduate
school in the Chicago area. During this time we frequently met on Friday nights, usually exhausted from the week.
Our first agenda was to go eat a good meal together.
Afterward we would take long walks and pour out our
hearts in prayers. During those Friday nights the Lord
taught me some special lessons about prayer.

I experienced the same help in college when a group
of students would meet each day before lunch. Then as a
student in graduate school, I found great aid from the
prayer meeting I hosted each night in my dorm room. The

graduate program I teach at Moody requires each student, staff person, and faculty member to have a prayer partner to assist them in their own personal prayer lives. Each student is also required to be a part of a small group each semester that is under the direction of a faculty member. Would you say that some of the most precious fellowship you have experienced in church has been in united and genuine prayer? I have such fond memories of a small church plant where every week we devoted our entire Sunday evening service to prayer.

As Jesus faced the crisis of going to the cross, He chose to face it with His closest human associates to "keep watch" with Him in prayer (Matthew 26:37–38). Even though they let Him down, the principle of companionship is certainly upheld. The Bible clearly affirms the blessing and need of godly companionship. "Iron sharpens iron, so one man sharpens another" (Proverbs 27:17). Further,

> *Two are better than one because they have a good return for their labor. For if either of them falls, the one will lift up his companion. But woe to the one who falls when there is not another to lift him up. Furthermore, if two lie down together they keep warm, but how can one be warm alone? And if one can overpower him who is alone, two can resist him. A cord of three strands is not quickly torn apart.* (Ecclesiastes 4:9–12)

In this chapter, we will explore one specific way that this companionship can aid your prayer life.

CASTING YOUR CARES UPON THE LORD

I have already stated that our anxieties are a significant means that God uses to draw us into prayer (Philippians 4:6–7). Jesus told His perplexed and troubled disciples that He wanted to give them His peace. In John 14:27 He says, "Peace I leave with you; My peace I give to you; not as the world gives do I give to you. Do not let your heart be troubled, nor let it be fearful."

Jesus' peace is referred to as "My peace" not only because He authored it and gives it, but also because He experienced it. In the midst of all the pressures of His life, He exhibited supernatural peace. He continually felt the pressure of all the expectations of those around Him and the pain of being rejected by His people and the religious leaders. He woke up each day knowing that there was a plot to kill Him and also that eventually one of His own disciples would betray and the rest would desert Him. Where many people go to find comfort in such stress is their family. Yet Jesus' family did not understand Him! In all of these circumstances He experienced a peace from His heavenly Father that He desired to leave with His followers.

The apostle Peter observed this peace, and under the inspiration of the Spirit he instructed God's people of all ages to cast their cares upon the Lord (I Peter 5:7). Such an instruction flows from the very heart of God and is found throughout the Bible. The psalmist had gone through the burden of being rejected by an intimate friend when he wrote in Psalm 55:22, "Cast your burden upon the Lord and He will sustain you; He will never allow the righteous to be shaken."

As we seek to cast our cares upon the Lord we need to be alert to the times that God desires to work through others to aid us. There are times that we need others to pray with us and for us in order to experience the peace Jesus gives. For this reason God instructs us to help bear each other's burdens (Galatians 6:2). One way to do this is in prayer.

HELP IN CASTING YOUR
CARES UPON THE LORD

As I sought God in prayer one day I diligently tried to get in touch with my troubled heart. I struggled and prayed all morning. I "limped" to my one o'clock class that I was to teach that Wednesday afternoon. After feebly attempting to lecture for a few minutes, I stopped and told the class that I was struggling with a burden that I had not been able to identify. I asked if they would pray for me. They graciously did, and after their prayer I continued the lecture with a new spiritual strength. When I returned to my office after class and sat at my desk, the burden I was carrying became immediately clear to me. God had worked through the prayers of others to aid me first in identifying and then in casting this care upon the Lord.

After a long and satisfying single life I married Penny

at age thirty-six. Less than two years later God gave us our first child, William Reynolds. He was followed by Michael Scott. I was so joyful to have these two gifts, but since I was approaching my mid-forties I felt that our quiver was full. But I also sensed that Penny and I were not in full agreement. She mainly just talked to the Lord about it and put no pressure on me. For some reason the thought of another child was a very fearful thought. Children are a "gift of the Lord" (Psalm 127:3). However, this passage goes on to say the "children of one's youth" (Psalm 127:4), and I felt that I was no longer a youth!

As I was up in the middle of the night praying, I decided to submit this fear to the elders of the church and have them pray with me. So I called the next day and arranged for this to happen. The elders graciously identified with my fears and very mercifully prayed for me without the slightest sense of condemnation. After their prayer I was free from the fear and was at complete peace at putting this matter in the Lord's hand.

Several months later Penny informed me she was pregnant. A few days earlier God had laid upon my heart a verse of Scripture that prepared me. Truly I rejoiced in God's goodness and His gracious gift. One of the elders began to call me "Abraham." The day David Preston was dedicated to the Lord I wept with tears of joy. Many times I have looked at him and recalled the time of prayer with the elders. I would not have this precious third son apart from the help afforded by godly companions in prayer.

10

Achieving Victories You Never Thought Were Possible

Prayer fills man's emptiness with God's fullness.

❧E. M. BOUNDS

My courtship story is quite long and humbling. I first met Penny in March of 1982, and one month later I asked the Lord to give her to me as my wife. God did answer that prayer, but not immediately—it was almost a seven-year wait. At a crucial point I called ten people who knew me and loved me and ask them to pray for our courtship. The requested intercession was not to try to persuade God of my desire but to gain needed direction. God honored the intercession of these dear friends. I believe this area of discerning God's will of a mate is too big for any one of us. You may be seeking the Lord with all your heart for an important decision, but it is wise to seek the intercession and counsel of godly people to confirm His direction.

Whatever your need or crisis, it is wise to follow the pattern in Scripture of informing your friends and requesting the compassion of our wonderful God in prayer. This is what Daniel did in his need.

> *Then Daniel went to his house and informed his friends, Hananiah, Mishael and Azariah, about the matter, so that they might request compassion from the God of heaven concerning this mystery, so that Daniel and his friends would not be destroyed with the rest of the wise men of Babylon.* (Daniel 2:17–18)

This is also what Peter and John did when they were threatened by the governing authorities.

> *When they had been released, they went to their own companions and reported all that the chief priests and the elders had said to them. And when they heard this, they lifted their voices to God with one accord.* (Acts 4:23–24a)

What do you do when you have a strong desire for something? Do you have a long enough track record to realize that not every strong urge is to be trusted? At the time of this deep desire it is tempting to think, *If God is really good, this is what He must do. And if He does not, He really does not have my best interests in mind.* I have learned to discuss these desires with others and ask them to intercede for me.

During my single adult years, if I ever considered initiating a relationship with a young lady, I would first request prayer from my mother and a few select companions. Many times God used their prayers to stop me from any action. God gave a wisdom from their prayers that never could have been received by only listening to my emotions. The Lord's restraints were not to frustrate me but only to preserve me for the person that He would provide in His perfect timing.

Trials and irritations can be signals to seek companionship in prayer. God can use the intercessions of others to lift the burden of a trial. But God may also lift the burden by changing our perspective. Wisdom is seeing life from God's point of view. It is discerning what good God desires to bring out of something that is not good in and of itself.

The prayers of others brought comfort to a woman who had been abused as a child. At the culmination of a long process she exclaimed, "Now I see how I can love Jesus in a new way. He was a completely innocent victim who was abused. He fully understands me and perhaps I can identify with Him in a way that others cannot." God used the prayers of others not to change the event but to give her perspective and interpretation of the event.

During the last forty days of my graduate school training for the ministry, the Lord laid it on a fellow student's heart to use the time for special prayer. For these forty days, six of us met for two hours before breakfast to pray and seek God. It was an international group; one brother was from India, another from Australia. Others were on the verge of going to the mission field. I was preparing to go into a doctoral program for further studies. There was "spiritual energy" in this prayer meeting that never could have been generated alone. It was a special way to end this phase of our training and be launched into our next steps of ministry.

Through the help of others we can achieve heights of prayer that we could not achieve alone. After lecturing on prayer for a week to a group of delightful missionaries in Taiwan, I rode on a bus with my missionary host, Will, to the airport. I was very tired, but Will and I began to pray and pour out our hearts together. It was a delightful hour of prayer that could never have been experienced without the stimulation of his companionship.

I will close this chapter with three simple and potentially life-changing suggestions:

1. Ask God for a "soul partner(s)." A soul partner is one with whom you feel free to share the innermost burden of your heart.

2. If you are married, seek to cultivate this with your spouse. This will require your working through any past bitterness that hinders true oneness of spirit. Do not get discouraged if the oneness is not achieved in one day, because it will take time. Focus on your responsibility and do not try to change your mate.

3. Make prayer a point of your life with others. Make it a practice to end your times of fellowship with others in prayer. If you have had people in your home, ask them before they leave, "How can we be praying for you?" Have a time of prayer right then when possible, and include the children.

I recall a dear pastor, Pastor Hovey, who very skillfully would end his phone conversations with his parishioners in prayer. I felt loved in a special way as Pastor Hovey would pray for me on the phone. Ask the Lord for many other ideas for genuine prayer to become part of your daily life.

The Help of Scripture

*There is only one way to maintain proper
motivation and direction in prayer. Here is the
way and also the open secret to true prosperity.*

Learning George Mueller's Secret

*I have joyfully dedicated my whole life to
the object of exemplifying how much
may be accomplished by prayer and faith.*

&-GEORGE MUELLER

George Mueller prayed he would live and work in such
a way as to be convincing proof that God hears
prayer and that it is always safe to trust in Him. Spanning
from 1805 to 1898, Mueller's life was filled with numerous accomplishments. He formed the Scriptural Knowledge Institute for Home and Abroad in 1834. He also
raised more than five million dollars through prayer, cared
for more than ten thousand orphans, gave away more than
two million Scriptures and Scripture portions, sent more
than one million dollars to missions, and wrote more than
three thousand letters a year. Between the ages of seventy-
one and eighty-five he engaged in a series of mission tours
in Europe, Asia, and America, which took him to forty-
five countries to evangelize the lost and encourage the believers.

Mueller's greatest accomplishment was no doubt the hundreds of lives that he inspired to believe God. One such person was J. Hudson Taylor, whose acquaintance with Mueller challenged him to found the China Inland Mission.

Mueller's primary purpose for the founding of the orphanages was not the physical and spiritual welfare of the orphans but showing the world that God was a prayer-answering God. He was burdened when he saw older believers paralyzed by the fear that God would forsake them in their twilight years. He felt for the younger men and women who sensed that they needed to compromise their integrity in order to "get ahead" and care for their families. He observed that their obsession to work such long hours not only injured their bodies but also robbed them of any time to refresh their souls and truly care for their families spiritually.

Mueller's own conviction was to make the financial needs of his ministry known only to God. Although all may not share this conviction, everyone can rejoice in the testimony of God's great faithfulness. In his lifetime, Mueller documented more than fifty thousand answers to prayer.[1] He learned to look to God alone for his needs in childlike faith. His biographer stated that he was never so fully a child in relationship to his heavenly Father as when he was ninety-three years old.[2]

The secret to Mueller's faith cannot be found in his background. By the age of ten he was a habitual thief and was later imprisoned for running up debts and not paying his bills. He chose to study to be a clergyman only because his father encouraged it as a prestigious vocation. In this time of study he was gloriously converted at a small gathering of believers. At this meeting the sight of a grown man on his knees praying for God's blessing revealed to him the reality of the living God. The secret to Mueller's faith cannot be found in his background, but rather in the grace of God that taught him the infinite value of communion with his heavenly Father and the use of a key spiritual discipline.

In the first four years of George Mueller's Christian life, he spent more time reading the works of men than the Scriptures. Up until the day of his conversion he could not even recall reading one chapter of the Book of books. However, in the ninety-second year of his life he told his biographer that for every page he had read in any other book he was sure that he had proportionately read ten pages of the Bible.[3] During the last twenty years of his life he read through the Scripture four or five times annually. In studying Mueller's life I have discovered that his devotion and delight in God's Word was the secret to his faith and life of prayer.

The greatest priority of Mueller's life was his communion with God. He writes:

> Friends often say, "I have so much to do, so many people to see, I cannot find time for Scripture study." Perhaps there are not many who have more to do than I. For more than half a century I have never known a day when

I had not more business than I could get through. For 4 years I had annually about 3,000 letters, and most of these have passed through my own hands.

Then, as pastor of a church with 1,200 believers, great has been my care. Besides, I have had charge of five immense orphanages; also, at my publishing depot, the printing and circulating of millions of tracts, books and Bibles; but I have always made it a rule never to begin work until I have had a good season with God and His Word.[4]

Mueller believed that one hour of prayer and four hours of work was far more productive than five hours of work. What did Mueller do in his time alone with God? If you ever come across a short booklet called "Soul Nourishment First," buy it. This booklet describes his practice of his priority of reading the Scripture and meditating upon a truth that would "hit" him until out of his study a prayer would flow from his heart. His primary business every day was to make his "soul happy in the Lord."

D. L. Moody said that he prayed to be a man of faith. He prayed for faith and prayed for faith as if faith would come down and strike him like lightning one day. Then he noticed the truth found in Romans 10:17 that faith comes from hearing the Word of God. Moody stated that he had been praying for faith with a closed Bible, but after reading Romans 10:17 he began to pray for faith with an open Bible, and his faith began to grow as never before.

R. A. Torrey said that "the prayer that is born of meditation upon the Word of God is the prayer that soars upward most easily to God's listening ears." Look at the amazing promise that God gives to the discipline of meditation of His Scriptures:

> *This book of the law shall not depart from your mouth, but you shall meditate on it day and night, so that you may be careful to do according to all that is written in it; for then you will make your way prosperous, and then you will have success. Have I not commanded you? Be strong and courageous! Do not tremble or be dismayed, for the Lord your God is with you wherever you go.* (Joshua 1:8–9)

> *But his delight is in the law of the Lord, and in His law he meditates day and night. He will be like a tree firmly planted by streams of water, which yields its fruit in its season and its leaf does not wither; and in whatever he does, he prospers.* (Psalm 1:2–3)

> *But one who looks intently at the perfect law, the law of liberty, and abides by it, not having become a forgetful hearer but an effectual doer, this man will be blessed in what he does.* (James 1:25)

In the next three chapters we will examine how to make the practice of meditation a reality in one's life.

Experiencing True Prosperity

If you abide in Me, and My words
abide in you, ask whatever you
wish, and it will be done for you.

⟩ JOHN 15:7

One day a former student we will call Tom opened up to me about a very private moral struggle in his life. The next week we spent much of a day together as I related to him everything that had ever helped me in dealing with temptation. He wrote down the insights, and we had a time of prayer together. As he left in his car I started walking to a nearby restaurant. It was located less than a mile from my apartment, and in my single years I often frequented it. On the walk to the restaurant I sensed a prayer burden of an intensity that I had never experienced up to that time in my life. All I could think of was two of the requests found in the prayer of Ephesians 1:15–23. I felt a great compulsion to pray that the Lord would give Tom "hope" and "power" in his struggle. I felt driven to pray this for him for about thirty minutes as I circled the block around the restaurant. In my flesh I wanted to eat and not pray, but I continued to pray until I felt the freedom in my spirit to stop. I abandoned my plan to eat and walked back to my apartment. I desired to call Tom that night, but I waited until the next day.

As I talked to Tom on the phone, I related to him the intense burden that I had felt on my walk to the restaurant. I asked him, "What was happening to you at that time?" He began to chuckle and responded that at that hour God began to show him the deep despair he had concerning his struggle. He also found a book on his bookshelf by Mark Bubeck and began to pray in the authority of the blood of Christ concerning his struggle. He now goes back to this evening as the beginning of the "breakthrough" when the Lord replaced his despair with "hope" and "power" in his weakness. In his ministry as a missionary and a pastor Tom has been used of God to help many others find hope in their struggles.

Meditation is simply talking to God about His Word with a desire that your life and those you pray for come into agreement with it. This is my definition of meditation, and it can be easily applied to any life. God used my exposure to Tom's need to trigger my memory of Ephesians 1:15–23, and this was the basis of my intercession for him.

Meditation is taking seriously Jesus' word, "If you abide in Me, and My words abide in you, ask whatever you wish, and it will be done for you" (John 15:7). In meditation we see the vital link between the discipline of Scriptures and the discipline of prayer. Without prayer the study of Scripture can turn into a merely intellectual exercise. Prayer without Scripture will lack needed motivation and guidance.

An older single man who had been on the mission field for many years came to the secular university campus and began teaching Bible studies. He was an unusual person, but a friend of mine had the wisdom to seek out this older man in order to learn from him. My friend would take walks with him and ask him many questions about the Bible. When asked about a difficult verse, the missionary one day responded and said, "I've been asking God for twenty-five years to open up that verse to me." Such a response was outside my paradigm at that time. When I was in my twenties I felt great discouragement if I could not understand a passage after devoting serious study to it. One needs to take seriously the need to prayerfully seek God in order to understand the Bible in a way that leads to an experience of its truth. This older gentleman had learned this lesson, and his prayerful response to the Scripture reflected this knowledge.

J. B. Lightfoot was one of the greatest Greek scholars of the nineteenth century. He said that in the final analysis there was only one way to learn the Scriptures, and that was through prayer. In other words he was saying that to know in one's experience what it meant to "walk by the Spirit" and "delight in the Lord" is only possible as one looks to the Lord in prayer.[1] When concentrated times of Bible study and Bible teaching such as seminary education are not done in a spirit of prayer, it can be very dangerous spiritually. One can get so used to talking about God that he neglects the habit of talking to God.

Graham Scroggie said that "prayer is an instinct of the soul but how to pray can only be learned from the inspired Scriptures." Let us take for example the area of prayer for our unsaved friends and relatives. The typical evangelistic prayer focuses on praying for the lost. This is certainly appropriate, but the clear emphasis in Scripture is to pray in a different direction. Jesus' burden for the lost multitude resulted in His instruction to pray that the Lord would send laborers into the harvest field (Matthew 9:38). In His deep burden for the unsaved He commanded prayer for the saints instead of the sinner. Likewise, the apostle Paul requested prayer for both the opportunity to witness (Colossians 4:3) and the courage to present the gospel (Ephesians 6:19–20). To pray for our lost friends is a naturally loving instinct, but it is God's Word that guides us how to do so. It instructs us to pray that the Lord would send someone into their lives who would have the opportunity and the freedom to clearly present the gospel.

The Scripture encourages us and motivates us to pray. Look at how God's promise to David in 2 Samuel 7:27 encouraged him to pray. For the last thirty-plus years I have found it helpful to begin my day by systematically reading the Bible and giving God the opportunity to direct my attention to certain truths. These truths become the springboard to begin speaking to the Lord.

One can even take a command, a promise, a statement, or a warning and turn it into prayer. I use the command of Ephesians 5:16 to "mak[e] the most of your time" to petition God to aid me as I approach certain opportunities. "Lord, left to myself I would squander this opportunity, but give me the grace for Your glory to make full use of it."[2] The statement of Ephesians 2:4 that declares God to be "rich in mercy" is a springboard to beseech the Lord for His merciful support in numerous situations. The Scripture provides the stimulation and guidance we need to *sustain* a meaningful prayer life.

When I came to the point of realizing my weakness in prayer, I began to make progress. It is our weakness that not only draws us to the Lord, causing us to depend on the Holy Spirit in prayer, but also to go to God's Word to show us how to express our hearts in prayer. We are so weak that God has condescended to give us the very words for praying.

Some of the most direct guidance one can receive is from the Psalms. A number of years ago I did a study of the Psalms for the express purpose of finding portions of Scripture to aid me in communicating the desire of my heart to God. For example, in regard to petitioning God for encouragement, listen to Psalm 86:4–5:

> *Make glad the soul of Your servant, for to You, O Lord, I lift up my soul. For You, Lord, are good, and ready to forgive, and abundant in lovingkindness to all who call upon You.*

Another example is the use of Psalm 17:8 for protection: "Keep me as the apple of the eye; hide me in the shadow of Your wings." In chapter 14 we will look at the use of other Scripture prayers.

13

Learning How to Pray for Christlike Growth

The Child continued to grow and
become strong, increasing in wisdom;
and the grace of God was upon Him.

≈ LUKE 2:40

When my wife, Penny, was pregnant with our first child, I was preparing to teach a class on the life of Christ. My life circumstances gave me a special interest in the birth narratives that are found in chapters 1 and 2 of Luke's gospel. My heart also yearned to know about the childhood of Christ. For this reason I found myself pondering the text of Luke 2:41–52.

In this passage I observed a number of characteristics of maturity in the boy Jesus. I saw how Jesus had a desire to learn. In fact, in this time of separation from His family and relatives, He manifested wisdom in the way He used His time. He also exhibited an ability to converse with adults by being able to be an attentive listener and an active learner who asked and even answered questions.

Modern American childhoods are characterized by a lack of interest in learning, a poor use of time, and an inability to relate to adults, but the culture Jesus grew up in reflected a more deliberate training of the young, and Jesus made good use of it.

In this snapshot of Jesus' life at age twelve, one also observes a youth who was faithful to His parents even when they were not looking. It was characterized by an obedience to His earthly parents (v. 51). His life was also characterized by an understanding that amazed others (v. 47).

After observing Luke 2:41–52, I was drawn back to the verse that preceded this passage. I saw in Luke 2:40 how God grew up His Son. Luke 2:41–52 seemed to be evidence of His human growth and development. It is here that I found some direction in praying for my own needed growth as well as the child whose birth I was anticipating.

The Lord's growth is described in three ways.

SPIRITUAL STRENGTH

First, it says that He became strong. The word that is translated "became strong" is the same one that is used in Luke 1:80 of John the Baptist's development. In Luke 1:80 we find the words "become strong in spirit." In fact, some manuscripts have "in spirit" after the verb in Luke 2:40. The phrase shows that physical strength is not the primary emphasis of the verb in this context. It is rather the strengthening of the human spirit.

Every person is created with a spirit. It is one of the aspects of man being made in God's image. When a person becomes a Christian, the spirit is made alive (Romans 8:10). This act of spiritual resurrection from a spirit that is dead to one that is alive is called "regeneration." God's desire is not only to make the spirit alive but also to strengthen it. While Christ's human spirit was never dead, He did have the capacity for growth and development in His spirit.

In Ephesians 3:14–19 one can find an inscripturated prayer for praying for our loved ones and ourselves to become strong in spirit. The Greek word for "strengthened" in Ephesians 3:16 is the same one that is used in Luke 2:40. It is the Holy Spirit who does the strengthening of our spirit or inner man. We see that His strengthening results in Christ's dwelling in our hearts. "Dwell" is not the same as the initial indwelling of Christ in the life of every believer at salvation. It is, rather, His controlling influence. The difference is the one between the initial indwelling of the Spirit and the filling of the Spirit (Romans 8:9; Ephesians 5:18). The result of Christ's dwelling or controlling one's heart is the ability to comprehend and experience all the dimensions of God's love. Christ longs to control us in order to allow us to experience His love.

INCREASE IN WISDOM

The second aspect of the child Christ's growth in Luke 2:40 was His increasing in wisdom. *Wisdom* is a very pregnant term in Scripture. It is hard to sum up in a single definition. I have found three definitions to offer some help.

One is "seeing life from God's point of view." This viewpoint can transform our responses to the trials and irritations that we encounter daily in our lives.

A second definition is the "ability to select the best goals for one's life and the best means to achieve them." Wisdom is God showing us where to go and how to get there.

A third definition is the "skill of living life before God." There is not only a skill in the doing of tasks such as carpentry, but also in living life. There is a skill in handling money, using our tongues, and relating to the people in our lives.

All three of these definitions are involved in the biblical concept of God's wisdom. A life that is characterized by wisdom brings great joy to those who care about us, and the lack of it brings grief (Proverbs 17:21, 25).

In Colossians 1:9 we find another inscripturated prayer that relates to the idea of growing in wisdom. It is prayer to be filled or controlled with the knowledge of what God desires us to be and do. This is true spiritual wisdom that will reflect itself in the behavior of one's life (Colossians 1:10, cf. James 3:13). Prayer is one way to receive God's wisdom (James 1:5).

GOD'S GRACE

The third aspect of Jesus' growth according to Luke 2:40 is the grace of God being upon Him. God's grace speaks of His favor. It also speaks more specifically of

God's enablement. We see this clearly in I Corinthians 15:10, "But by the grace of God I am what I am, and His grace toward me did not prove vain; but I labored even more than all of them, yet not I, but the grace of God with me."

Paul said that grace was the secret to His labor. It refers to the gracious work of the Spirit who provides the motivation and enablement we need to do God's will (cf. Philippians 2:13). This definition explains Paul's exhortations to Timothy in 2 Timothy 2:1—"Be strong in the grace that is in Christ Jesus."

The believer is commanded to grow in grace in 2 Peter 3:18. We are exhorted to come boldly to the throne of grace and receive His mercy and grace to help us in our need (Hebrews 4:16). Such a prayer presupposes a humility in one's life that is willing to deal with any point of resistance (James 4:6). God even provides providential circumstances to aid us in experiencing more of His grace according to 2 Corinthians 12:7–10.

The Epistles characteristically contain the opening greetings of grace and peace. This is a prayer that the believers in these churches continually experience God's grace. A true believer has already experienced the grace of God that leads to salvation (Ephesians 2:8–9). However, every believer is in need of the grace of God for daily living (I Corinthians 15:10). We can continually look to God for His provision for motivation and enablement to do what He has called us to do.

Nothing is a greater joy in my life than the privilege of knowing Jesus. Next to this is the joy of having a wife and three sons. But probably nothing makes me feel more inadequate than my family responsibilities. In this marvelous little verse—Luke 2:40—I've found comfort and direction in praying to God for my family. I'm glad that I can introduce my boys to a God who truly is a perfect Father. I know that He alone can strengthen their spirit, give them His wisdom, and supply them with His grace.

Let your inadequacy draw you to God in prayer, and believe Him for these three prayer requests for your life and for the lives of those you love.

14

Learning to
Pray Scripture

The key is to pray according to God's will. To
know His will we must know His thoughts.
To know His thoughts we must saturate our
minds with His word. Then we will begin to
experience the authority of God in our prayers.

❧ CHARLES HENLEY

I am very grateful to the administration of the Moody
Graduate School, which has allowed me to teach a course
on "The Theology and Practice of Prayer." The first time I
taught this class I read a number of books on prayer as I
prepared the lectures. However, the greatest help did not
come from these excellent books but rather from the Scriptures themselves. The most significant aid came from going
through the Bible and praying the prayers of Scripture.

I began to see the treasure of these scriptural prayers
while first teaching the Prison Epistles. God gave me the
privilege to teach this course about fifteen times. It was
during these years that the prayers of Ephesians 1:15–23;
3:14–21; Philippians 1:9–11; and Colossians 1:9–12 became very precious to me.

The first step in effectively using a scriptural prayer is to cognitively understand it. One day I was lecturing on the book of Ephesians and teaching on one of these prayers. When I got back to my office I thought, *What does that prayer really mean?* On the one hand I knew what it meant because I had carefully studied it. On the other hand, I did not know what it really meant because I had not spent sufficient time praying it to the Lord. The first step is to understand the passage, but this is only the foundation.

The second step in effectively using a scriptural prayer is to pray it to the Lord. If one could understand a scriptural prayer without praying it, he would not be fully using that part of God's Word. If one could presume to teach another person a scriptural prayer without the learner ever praying it, once again the fullest intent of that passage of Scripture could be aborted.

For a period of about six months I prayed the four prayers of Ephesians 1:15–23; 3:14–21; Philippians 1:9–11; and Colossians 1:9–12 to the Lord for myself and several other people. During this time these prayers became precious to me. At first I felt "clumsy" as I used them, but after a time they became part of my life. We will briefly look at each one.

EPHESIANS 1:15–23

For this reason I too, having heard of the faith in the Lord Jesus which exists among you and your love for all the saints, do not cease giving thanks for you, while making mention of you in my prayers; that the

> *God of our Lord Jesus Christ, the Father of glory, may give to you a*
> *spirit of wisdom and of revelation in the knowledge of Him. I pray*
> *that the eyes of your heart may be enlightened, so that you will know*
> *what is the hope of His calling, what are the riches of the glory of His*
> *inheritance in the saints, and what is the surpassing greatness of His*
> *power toward us who believe. These are in accordance with the work-*
> *ing of the strength of His might which He brought about in Christ,*
> *when He raised Him from the dead and seated Him at His right*
> *hand in the heavenly places, far above all rule and authority and*
> *power and dominion, and every name that is named, not only in this*
> *age but also in the one to come. And He put all things in subjection*
> *under His feet, and gave Him as head over all things to the church,*
> *which is His body, the fullness of Him who fills all in all.*

This prayer follows the praise of Ephesians 1:3–14.
After Paul praised God for giving the believer every spiritual blessing, he prayed for the believers in Ephesus. How
do you pray for people who already have everything? The
prayer is for spiritual enlightenment, that God would give
them a spirit or disposition to understand His revelation
and receive His wisdom. "Spirit" is used in the way it is
used in 2 Timothy 1:7, where God declares that he has not
given us a "spirit of timidity." A spirit of wisdom and revelation will result in a more intimate knowledge of God
and the eyes of one's heart being enlightened.

This enlightenment will lead to an experiential
knowledge of three things. The first is a life of hope that
is based on the truth that God has called them into a relationship with Himself. There is nothing as powerful as
praying hope into one's own life and the lives of others. It

is the opposite of despair. One can be tempted to despair in all of life or in an area of life. God desires to uproot this despair and replace it with hope.

The second thing that Paul prays for the believer to know in his experience is the "riches of the glory of His inheritance among the saints." If you met somebody who introduced himself as having the last name of Rockefeller, you would probably suspect that the person is rich. However, since God is the Father of every Christian, the believer possesses even more infinite wealth and has an even richer and more glorious inheritance! God also calls His people His inheritance (Psalm 94:14). It is one way that He communicates to us that we are His treasured ones.

The third thing that Paul prays for the believer to know is God's power. This was the pursuit of Paul. It is hard to pray for someone else to attain something that we have no interest in ourselves (Philippians 3:10). This power is described in three ways. The first is resurrection power, which is the power that gives victory over sin and death. It is also the power that gives victory out of apparent defeat, which we discussed in chapter 4. The second description of this power is the ascension of Christ. Here, He was seated above "all rule and authority and power and dominion" (Ephesians 1:21). This is the authority that the believer draws upon in his spiritual battles (Ephesians 6:10–12). The third description is the power that subjected all things to Christ as the Head of the church. The experience of this power is found by looking to His fullness to meet all our needs and inadequacies.

Ephesians 1:15–23 is a prayer that the believer would realize his spiritual riches. It is a prayer that the believer would know a life of hope, realize His inheritance, and experience His power.

EPHESIANS 3:14–21

For this reason I bow my knees before the Father, from whom every family in heaven and on earth derives its name, that He would grant you, according to the riches of His glory, to be strengthened with power through His Spirit in the inner man, so that Christ may dwell in your hearts through faith; and that you, being rooted and grounded in love, may be able to comprehend with all the saints what is the breadth and length and height and depth, and to know the love of Christ which surpasses knowledge, that you may be filled up to all the fullness of God. Now to Him who is able to do far more abundantly beyond all that we ask or think, according to the power that works within us, to Him be the glory in the church and in Christ Jesus to all generations forever and ever. Amen.

This prayer is an appeal to God to grant or give us something. Let us always remember that prayer is asking God to do for us what we cannot do for ourselves. The appeal is to God's inexhaustible wealth or the riches of His glory.

The request is to be strengthened in our inner man. The result of the Spirit's strengthening is Christ's dwelling in the heart of the believer. The Spirit indwells every believer at the time of conversion (Romans 8:9). Although He is present in every believer, He is not always given full freedom to rule. This prayer assumes that the Spirit is present and prays for Him to fill the believer so that Christ's control would be evident in the believer's heart or control center.

The result of Christ's dwelling in one's heart is that the believer would comprehend and know in his experience all the dimensions of God's great love. Why does Christ desire to control the believer? This prayer provides the answer. It is so that He can love the believer. Who experiences the most love from a parent—the submissive child or the rebellious child? Christ, who is called "Eternal Father" (Isaiah 9:6), longs for you to experience every facet of His love. This will not happen when anger, guilt, and fear control your heart. Submit these battles to the Spirit and enthrone Christ on your heart. In so doing you are saying yes to His love and the fulfillment of His plan for you, which is spoken of as being "filled up to all the fullness of God." The prayer concludes with one of the greatest benedictions in all the Bible.

PHILIPPIANS 1:9–11

And this I pray, that your love may abound still more and more in real knowledge and all discernment, so that you may approve the things that are excellent, in order to be sincere and blameless until the day of Christ; having been filled with the fruit of righteousness which comes through Jesus Christ, to the glory and praise of God.

Prayed over Dave

The reference to this prayer is inscribed inside Penny's and my wedding rings. This is a prayer for abounding or growing love. It is a prayer that believers would so know God's love for them that they would respond in loving God and others in an ever-increasing way. Love is not primarily a feeling and therefore requires God's knowledge and discernment to know how to express it.

Life is filled with countless choices, and for that reason the request is that God would help us put our stamp of approval or choice on the most excellent ways to express our love. The fact that this is a prayer implies that we will never be able to make these correct choices apart from the help of God.

The final request envisions the believer standing before the Lord for his life to be evaluated. One who has lived a life of love will be sincere and blameless in God's evaluation. Verse 11 is a further description of this blameless life.

COLOSSIANS 1:9–12

For this reason also, since the day we heard of it, we have not ceased to pray for you and to ask that you may be filled with the knowledge of His will in all spiritual wisdom and understanding, so that you will walk in a manner worthy of the Lord, to please Him in all respects, bearing fruit in every good work and increasing in the knowledge of God; strengthened with all power, according to His glorious might, for the attaining of all steadfastness and patience; joyously giving thanks to the Father, who has qualified us to share in the inheritance of the saints in Light. This verse Prayed over Jessica

The one request of this prayer is to be filled or controlled with an experiential knowledge of what God desires. There is a difference in knowing a truth of God's will or desire and being controlled by this truth. The latter is described by Jesus when He spoke of His words abiding and living in us (John 15:7). Proverbs 7:1 describes it as "treasuring" His commandments in our heart.

Letting His truth control us is described as "walking worthy" or bringing honor to our Lord's name. It also results in giving pleasure to God, bearing fruit, and increasing in one's knowledge of God.

These are a few of the examples of prayers God has included in His Word to aid us in communicating with Him. When you know something is God's will, you can bring it to God in prayer with absolute confidence according to 1 John 5:14–15. The surest way to have this confidence is to pray with prayers of Scripture.[1]

> *This is the confidence which we have before Him, that, if we ask anything according to His will, He hears us. And if we know that He hears us in whatever we ask, we know that we have the requests which we have asked from Him.*

The Discipline
of Prayer

*Developing the discipline of prayer will
sooner or later lead to failure—here is hope.*

15

Realizing the Struggle of Prayer

*Devote yourselves to prayer, keeping alert
in it with an attitude of thanksgiving.*

❧ COLOSSIANS 4:2

The Bible reveals to us the schemes Satan uses to seek to harm God's people. One such scheme is his attempt to lead us "astray from the simplicity and purity of devotion to Christ" (2 Corinthians 11:3). Don Currin alludes to this scheme when he writes:

> Satan called a worldwide convention. In the opening address to his evil spirits he said, "We can't keep true Christians from going to church. We can't keep them from reading their Bibles and knowing the truth. We can't even keep them from having conservative values. But we can do something else. We can keep them from forming an intimate, abiding experience with Christ. If they gain that connection with Jesus, our power over them is broken. So let them go to church, read their Bibles, and have their conservative lifestyles, but steal

their time so they do not have time to have an intimate fellowship with Christ. This is what I want you to do: keep them busy in the non-essentials of life and invent innumerable schemes to occupy their minds."[1]

This is so true. We get busy then have no time. we must stand firm

According to Deuteronomy 10:13, God's commandments are for our good! God has graciously commanded and given us a pattern for the discipline of prayer in Scripture.

Devote yourselves to prayer, keeping alert in it with an attitude of thanksgiving. (Colossians 4:2)

Now when Daniel knew that the document was signed, he entered his house (now in his roof chamber he had windows open toward Jerusalem); and he continued kneeling on his knees three times a day, praying and giving thanks before his God, as he had been doing previously. (Daniel 6:10)

But we will devote ourselves to prayer and to the ministry of the word. (Acts 6:4)

Most of our lives are overextended, and we fail to grasp that if our service does not flow from an abiding relationship with Christ, it is the fruit of our flesh and not of the Spirit. Hudson Taylor warned of this long ago when he said, "As wounds when healed often leave a scar, so the sin of neglected communion may be forgiven and yet the effect remain permanently."

The devil is called a "thief" (John 10:10), and he has robbed many of us in our generation of our most precious commodity—time. He has often used the television, which most families view by the hours, to be our place of rest rather than learning to find true rest in cultivating Christ's fellowship. Christian researcher George Barna reported that born-again Christians spend seven times more time watching television than participating in Bible reading, prayer, and worship.[2]

The knowledge explosion produces another challenge. With so much information—even "good" and "godly" input—to process, there is little time spent on meditation, which results in true prayer, as we discussed in chapter 12.

We are all faced with a great challenge. In a survey conducted by the Asian Research Center in Manila and sent to eight hundred missionaries, the problem of maintaining a systematic devotional time was identified as their greatest spiritual struggle. No other problem even came close to this one in the study.

Cultivating meaningful disciplines in our lives *is* a struggle, and if a person has never known anything of a struggle there is likely a lack of depth in the person's development. The words of Pastor J. Sidlow Baxter are quite instructive. When he entered the ministry, he started each morning with a structured schedule that included ninety minutes for prayer and Bible study. But as time went by, sometimes administration and other pastoral duties crowded in. He persevered, but often failed, and repented with tears before the Lord. Then came the crisis. It was time for prayer. But a pile of letters waited to be answered, and answering them seemed more "practical" than praying. And he fought with a voice that insisted the letters were too urgent to be put off.

It said, "Look here, Sid, don't you think the Lord knows all the busy occupations which are taking your time? . . . You're converted. You're born again. You're in the ministry. People are proud of you, and you are having conversions. Doesn't that show that God is pleased with you? And even if you can't pray, don't worry too much about it. Look, Sid, you better face up to it—you're not one of the spiritual ones." . . .

I don't want to use extravagant phrases but if you had plunged a dagger into my bosom, it couldn't have hurt me more. "Sid, you're not one of the spiritual ones."

I'm not the introspective type, but that morning I took a good look into Sidlow Baxter, and I found that there was an area of me that did not want to pray . . . but I looked more closely and found that there was a part of me that did. The part that didn't was the emotions, and the part that did was the intellect and the will. . . .

So will and I drag off those wretched emotions by the scruff of the neck, and we went to prayer. If you had asked me afterwards, "Did you have a good time?" do you think I could have said yes? A good time, no. It was a fight all the way. What I would have done without will, I don't know. In the middle of the most earnest intercessions I suddenly found that one of my principal emotions was away out on the golf course playing golf. And

I had to run out to the golf course and drag him back. And a few minutes later I found another one of my emotions traveled a day and half ahead and was preaching a sermon that I hadn't even prepared. . . .

This went on for about 2 ½ weeks, but will and I stuck it out. And then one morning during that third week I looked at my watch and said, "Will, it's time for prayers. You ready?" And will said, "Yes, I'm ready." And just as we were going in, I heard one of my chief emotions say to the others, "Come on fellows, there's no use wearing ourselves out, they'll go on no matter what we do."

Suddenly, one day while will and I were pressing our case at the throne of the heavenly glory one of the chief emotions shouted, "Hallelujah!" and all the other emotions said, "Amen!" For the first time the whole territory of James Sidlow Baxter was happily coordinated in the exercise of prayer.[3]

16

Understanding Jesus' Patterns of Prayer

Not only does God command us to pray,
He permits us to pray. Prayer is both a
must and a may, an obligation and a gift.

☙ BEN PATTERSON

A friend of mine was eating dinner with his family in a restaurant in California. He looked over at a neighboring table and observed the people bowing in prayer. After he and his family had finished eating, he went over to the table to tell the people that their acknowledgment of the Lord was an encouragement to him. They replied, "Oh, we were not acknowledging the Lord. We are praying to Satan that he would discourage every pastor's wife."

Because there is so much at stake in this matter, let us go to the Master to observe His example. When did Jesus pray? Certainly He lived a lifestyle of prayer, but you also can observe definite patterns of prayer. Here are four distinct patterns that you can learn from the Gospels.

JESUS PRAYED BEFORE THE IMPORTANT EVENTS AND DECISIONS OF HIS LIFE

It was at this time that He went off to the mountain to pray, and He spent the whole night in prayer to God. And when day came, He called His disciples to Him and chose twelve of them, whom He also named as apostles. (Luke 6:12–13)

That Christ prayed in preparation for important events and decisions can be observed in His spending the night in prayer before the choosing of His disciples. This was one of the most crucial decisions of His life as it was the foundation of spreading His love to the world. As a naive college student I read Luke 6:12–13 and asked God how He would have me apply this. I thought of who I would ever influence or disciple. It occurred to me that if I ever got married my wife would be the person whom I would influence for better or worse. So I prayed that God would allow me to stay up all night before I proposed to the girl He would have me marry. I prayed this naive prayer in 1972. I never remembered it again until one night in July of 1988. I was at the very end of my courtship and I could not sleep. On that Wednesday night, July 13, 1988, I was reminded of the prayer I had prayed sixteen years earlier. It was not that I was so godly that I determined to pray all night. It was simply that I could not sleep and God brought back to my mind the prayer that I had forgotten but that had been treasured up in His throne room. I struggled and in my excitement prayed through the night, and the following Saturday the Lord arranged the opportunity to ask Penny to marry me (and she said "Yes"!).

JESUS PRAYED AFTER THE SIGNIFICANT ACHIEVEMENTS OF HIS LIFE

Immediately He made the disciples get into the boat and go ahead of Him to the other side, while He sent the crowds away. After He had sent the crowds away, He went up on the mountain by Himself to pray; and when it was evening, He was there alone. (Matthew 14:22–23)

After success is when it is easiest to be the most prayerless. Do you pray as much after the time of crisis or ministry as before the event? After He fed the multitude consisting of five thousand men aside from the women and children, He retreated into solitude to pray. The result was that He went from victory to victory as the Father prepared Him for the next miracle and ministry.

I have found it helpful to schedule special times of prayer after ministry responsibilities. These times provide opportunities both to reflect on how I might be more effective in the future and to follow up the ministry in prayer.

JESUS PRAYED WHEN LIFE WAS UNUSUALLY BUSY

In the early morning, while it was still dark, Jesus got up, left the

house, and went away to a secluded place, and was praying there.
(Mark 1:35)

Mark 1:35 occurs after the busiest recorded day in the life of Jesus. In the time of great ministry success and enormous response, His time alone with the Father provided Him guidance that would have never been derived from His circumstances. The guidance was to not remain in Capernaum but to go to the neighboring cities throughout Galilee.

Martin Luther's statement is often quoted, "I have so much to do that I must spend the first three hours in prayer." I frankly have seen it more often quoted than practiced! Perhaps such a statement ends up being a disservice to us because we feel like our experience in no way matches up to it.

When I surrendered my life to the Lord in college, time took on a new meaning to me. I developed a thirst to read and learn about ways to better manage my time. I went to the chairman of the department of management at Auburn University and asked him if I could do an independent study on the subject of time management. I told him that I would like to do it from a Christian perspective. Very graciously he gave me permission to do the study. I came to the conclusion that you do not "spend" time with God. You "invest" it. Time alone with Him can be one of the greatest time savers of your life.

It is in your time alone with the Lord that you can surrender the burden and the anxiety of the load to Him

(Philippians 4:6–7; I Peter 5:7). You can also find the perspective to be delivered from the truly nonessential things that often seem important. You can find new energy and ideas as you "commit your works to the Lord and your plans will be established" (Proverbs 16:3).

In my first year of teaching I felt like I needed to use every second to be working on the lectures for my courses, which were all new preparations. Being single at the time, I worked night and day. During the spring semester our school held an annual Bible conference in which regular classes were not conducted. Feeling the need to seize the opportunity, I anticipated putting together a number of lectures. It was in this first week of February 1981 that the Lord slowed me down to teach me a vital lesson. During this time I developed the solemn conviction that my approach to preparation needed a change.

The conviction I came to was that God would never give me so much to do that I could not accomplish it after having time with Him. I could give myself too much work to crowd this out, and others might even give me too much work, but the Lord would not do so. The conviction that the Lord gave was that I was to seek Him each day and let Him minister to me. From the overflow of His work in my needy life I would never lack the messages I needed to complete His ministry through me.

The discipline of time alone with God should not be looked at as another thing to put on your "to do" list. This attitude will only lead to resentment from the added pressure that it produces. It should be viewed as a gift from a gracious and kind God. He cares so much for you and me that He is not just interested in our accomplishments but also in shepherding our hearts.

In Jesus' humanity He had emotional limitations. In other words, He needed to get *refueled*, and it was through His time with His heavenly Father that this happened. In fact, the word for *praying* in Mark 1:35 does not primarily refer to intercession for others but to the outpouring of His own soul to the Father for renewal and refreshment.

The devotional life of Jesus is prophetically described in Isaiah 50:4–5. These verses portray the Father as awakening the Son each morning to listen to His encouraging messages. Jesus not only responded in personal obedience to the Father's input but overflowed with timely messages that sustain the weary. This is the picture of "abounding" and overflowing in the work of the Lord (1 Corinthians 15:58). It is in those times that the Lord in His humanity resisted His own temptation of discouragement.

John Hyde faced a crisis when he arrived in India and was assigned to language study. At first he neglected his own disciplines of prayer and Scripture but later returned to them as his first priority amidst some opposition even from other missionaries. However, history vindicates his enormously fruitful life, and he by no means neglected language study. He became a fluent speaker of three languages.

As you seek God first in your current life situation—in your ministry, career, and roles as student, mother, father, or grandparent—He will meet you with His wisdom. His yoke is not hard to wear and His load is light (Matthew 11:30). Do not fear to take the step of faith in seeking Him, for He will never make you irresponsible.

JESUS PRAYED WHEN HE WAS OVERWHELMED WITH NEED

Jesus was going through all the cities and villages, teaching in their synagogues and proclaiming the gospel of the kingdom, and healing every kind of disease and every kind of sickness. Seeing the people, He felt compassion for them, because they were distressed and dispirited like sheep without a shepherd. Then He said to His disciples, "The harvest is plentiful, but the workers are few. Therefore beseech the Lord of the harvest to send out workers into His harvest." (Matthew 9:35–38)

We will refer to these verses again in chapter 19. Section one of the book showed how the needs of our heart are a vital key to our prayer life. No one ever just decides to be a man or woman of prayer. God awakens people through their sense of needs. In this passage, our Lord's infinite sensitivity to the hurts of the crowd motivated His loving exhortation to His disciples to pray.

A busy pastor of a very large church told me that at the beginning of his year he took out his calendar and filled in his key appointments first. He said the most significant appointments that he put in were his appointments with God. With these on his calendar first, he was able to graciously decline other invitations and opportunities with the polite and truthful answer that he already had an appointment.

You may have a demanding schedule as a busy mother or a very stressful job, but rest assured that God understands your circumstances whatever they may be. There is nothing wrong with rescheduling an appointment. Notice that even the Lord did not get upset when His disciples came to Him during His devotions (Mark 1:35–38). We must remember that the goal is to develop a lifestyle of prayer in which we continually share our heart with God. The exact habits or forms will not be the same for every person. It is the lifestyle of prayer that General Stonewall Jackson talks about when he says,

> I have so fixed the habit in my mind that I never raise a glass of water to my lips without asking God's blessing, never seal a letter without putting a word of prayer under the seal, never take a letter from the post without a brief sending of my thoughts heavenward, never change my classes in the lecture room without a minute's petition for the cadets who go out and for those who come in.

It is Jesus Christ's sacrificial death alone that has purchased for us every spiritual blessing (Ephesians 1:3). In the discipline of prayer we put ourselves in a position to receive what He has graciously provided because He has chosen to work through prayer. In prayer your very life can bring great delight to God (Proverbs 15:8).

The Importance of Prayer

Knowing the importance of prayer may only discourage you—here is how to get beyond that discouragement.

Gaining Strength Through Prayer

When prayer is moved to the periphery of the
church, it can only mean that God has, too.

&·BEN PATTERSON

S teve Farrar relates a fascinating story about the life of
a man named George McCluskey.

> McCluskey was a man who decided to make a shrewd
> investment. As he married and started a family, he de-
> cided to invest one hour a day in prayer. He was con-
> cerned that his kids might follow Christ and establish
> their own homes where Christ was honored. After a
> time, he decided to expand his prayers to include not
> only his children, but their children and the children
> after them. Every day between 11 A.M. and noon, he
> would pray for the next three generations.
>
> As the years went by, his two daughters committed
> their lives to Christ and married men who went into
> full-time ministry. The two couples produced four girls
> and one boy. Each of the girls married a minister and
> the boy became a pastor. The first two children born to

this generation were both boys. Upon graduation from high school, the two cousins chose the same college and became roommates. During their sophomore year, one of the boys decided to go into ministry as well. The other one didn't. He knew the family history and undoubtedly felt some pressure to continue the family legacy by going into ministry himself, but he chose not to. In a manner of speaking, this young man became the black sheep of the family. He was the first one in four generations not to go into full-time Christian ministry.

He decided to pursue his interest in psychology and, over the years, met with success. After earning his doctorate, he wrote a book to parents that became a best-seller. He then wrote another and another, all best-sellers. Eventually he started a radio program that is now heard on more than a thousand stations each day. The black sheep's name? James Dobson, without a doubt the most influential and significant leader of the pro-family movement in America. His ministry is the direct result of the prayers of a man who lived four generations ago. [1]

Steve Farrar concluded by stating, "I don't know about you, but my family could sure use a black sheep like that."

Leroy Eims, a leader in the Navigators, spoke one day to a group of graduate students preparing for ministry about the subject of discipleship. Since he had spent much of his life discipling others and was looked upon as the expert in the field, we eagerly awaited his words when he stated that he would like to give us the four keys to discipleship. "They are (1) prayer; (2) prayer; (3) prayer; and (4) the Word. The disciples for whom I have been burdened to pour out my heart in prayer are the ones that have made the most significant impact on others."

How would you answer the following two questions?

True or False 1. To take time out of prayer and put it into service is a bad investment.

True or False 2. To take time out of service and put it into prayer is a way to reap an enormous gain.

Is it not true that we might give a "true" answer with our minds, but our lifestyle shout a resounding "false"? Many of us continue to make the mistake of trying to compensate for our lack of communion with God with increased social and spiritual activity.

Robert Murray McCheyne was a very godly Scottish minister who suffered physically. He urged others to give of themselves to prayer. "If you do not pray," he stated, "God will probably lay you aside from your ministry as he did me, to teach you to pray." His statement should not be taken as a threat but as an earnest plea that came from a heart of one whom God had graciously taught to pray. In fact Dr. Bill Bright, the founder of Campus Crusade for Christ, in the midst of his demanding ministry said that he longed for the day that he could be promoted from his job as president to the ministry of intercession.

As you study the lives of godly men and women you

will see that "prayer was no little habit tacked onto the periphery of their lives, it was their lives. It was the most serious work of their most productive years."[2]

It is often the case that the study of prayer and its importance only leads to discouragement because the prayer lives of some of these "spiritual giants" are so far beyond our experience that we despair after trying to imitate it for a short time. Should an occasional jogger despair after watching an Olympic marathon because he cannot match the athletes' performance the next day? Certainly not! And it would be equally unwise to be driven to despair rather than to be instructed, encouraged, and challenged by those who have been taught of God.

Realizing God's Desire to Bless You

The greatest thing anyone can do for
God and for man is to pray. It is not
the only thing. But it is the chief thing.

❧S. D. GORDON

O ur spiritual life is vitally linked to the experience of
true prayer. Oswald Chambers states it this way, "If
we think of prayer as the breath of our lungs and the
blood from our hearts, we think rightly. The blood flows
and the breathing continues—we are not conscious of it
but it is always going on." It is the kindness of God who
lovingly commands us to "pray without ceasing" (I Thessalonians 5:17). God's commands are for His glory *and*
our eternal good (Deuteronomy 10:13). The sin of
prayerlessness (compare I Samuel 12:23) brings great
harm to one's own life. The tragedy of not enjoying fellowship with God as one serves Him is what Don Currin
refers to as he relates this metaphor:

The story is told about a spring whose waters had certain medicinal properties so that those who drank from

it were helped in the cases of various infirmities. In the course of time, homes sprung up around the spring. Later, a hotel was built, then stores of all kinds. Eventually, a town grew into a city! Years passed. Then there came a day when visiting tourists would ask, "By the way, where is the spring from which this grew?" Dwellers of the city would rub their hands in embarrassment and say, "I am sorry that I cannot tell you, but somehow, in the midst of all our progress and improvement we lost the spring and no one knows where it is." Could it be that in the midst of all our ministerial progress we have lost the Spring from Whom it has grown?[1]

The most effective way I know how to communicate the nature and importance of true prayer is to realize that it all begins with an understanding of who God is. I give a more detailed view of the character of God in chapters 5–8 of my book *Living the Life God Has Planned*. It is God Himself who gave us His inspired revelation to teach us the importance of prayer.

Jesus also linked His exhortation to prayer with an accurate view of God:

Ask, and it will be given to you; seek, and you will find; knock, and it will be opened to you. For everyone who asks receives, and he who seeks finds, and to him who knocks it will be opened. Or what man is there among you who, when his son asks for a loaf, will give him a stone? Or if he asks for a fish, he will not give him a snake, will he? If you then, being evil, know how to give good gifts to your children, how much more will your Father who is in heaven give what is good to those who ask Him! (Matthew 7:7–11)

One of the most significant times of my own spiritual growth came when God more clearly illuminated my mind to see His kindness and goodness. This occurred at a week-long missions conference in Dallas, Texas. It was here that I realized my tendency to view God through the glasses of my guilty conscience rather than through the glasses of *Christ*. As Luis Palau spoke of God's grace in Guatemala, I realized I'd always seen God as One whose expectations I could never meet rather than One who truly desired to bless me. I could think of many reasons why He should never bestow His gifts on me. However, I began to see that I needed to simply humble myself before the Lord and receive from His kind hand the gracious gift that Christ has earned for me.

True prayer is a means of experiencing God's gifts.

- True prayer is the means of appropriating God's salvation.

  Whoever will call on the name of the Lord will be saved. (Romans 10:13)

- True prayer is the means of experiencing God's peace.

  Be anxious for nothing, but in everything by prayer and supplication with thanksgiving let your requests be made known to God. And the peace of God, which surpasses all comprehension, will guard your hearts and your minds in Christ Jesus. (Philippians 4:6–7)

- True prayer is a means of experiencing God's joy.

  *Until now you have asked for nothing in My name; ask and you
  will receive, so that your joy may be made full.*
  (John 16:24)

- True prayer is a means of the revival of God's
  people.

  *And [if] My people who are called by My name humble them-
  selves and pray and seek My face and turn from their wicked
  ways, then I will hear from heaven, will forgive their sin and will
  heal their land.*
  (2 Chronicles 7:14)

- True prayer is a means of receiving the gift of
  perseverance.

  *Now He was telling them a parable to show that at all times they
  ought to pray and not to lose heart.*
  (Luke 18:1)

To be sure, the unrepentant heart that spurns God's
kindness and grace will experience His judgment. However, the Lord even calls His judgment His unusual or ex-
traordinary work (Isaiah 28:21). In other words, God
yearns to bless *you* with His eternal best! He is even kind
to ungrateful and evil men (Luke 6:35). This is a verse for
which even I can qualify.

If we insist on having our own way, God will give it to
us. He encourages His redeemed people to open their
mouths and let Him graciously fill them. If His people refuse to listen to Him, He will give them over "to the stub-

bornness of their heart" (Psalm 81:12). However, notice the yearning with which He speaks to those who have *refused* to listen to Him and are under His loving discipline.

> *Oh that My people would listen to Me,* that Israel would walk in My ways! I would quickly subdue their enemies and turn My hand against their adversaries. Those who hate the Lord would pretend obedience to Him, and their time of punishment would be forever. But I would feed you with the finest of the wheat, and with honey from the rock I would satisfy you. (Psalm 81:13–16, italics added)

He still desires to bless His disobedient people and encourages their return to Him! In prayer we must humbly come to God and recognize that He is kind and good. We must view Him not as one who desires to withhold from us what is truly best but as One who earnestly yearns to bless us beyond our highest imagination.

Understanding How God Works

Prayer does not fit us for the greater
work; prayer is the greater work.

❧ OSWALD CHAMBERS

How does our kind and holy God accomplish His
work? His usual method is to place a prayer burden
on someone's heart. As a person prays in response to that
prayer burden, the work of God is set in motion. The sovereign God of the universe has chosen to work through
prayer. A. B. Simpson stated, "There is no wonder more
supernatural and divine in the life of a believer than the
mystery and the ministry of prayer . . . the hand of the
child touching the arm of the Father and moving the wheel
of the universe."

OUR ASSIGNED TASK

Let us look at some pertinent Scripture that reveals
God's method of working.

On your walls, O Jerusalem, I have appointed watchmen; all day and all night they will never keep silent. You who remind the Lord, take no rest for yourselves; and give Him no rest until He establishes and makes Jerusalem a praise in the earth. (Isaiah 62:6–7)

You will notice that true prayer begins with God. It is the Lord who encourages His people to take no rest for themselves as they remind Him of His promises in prayer. In fact He even tells them to give Him no rest until He does what He has promised to do! God is seen as both the initiator in giving the promise to His people and in encouraging His people to pray the promises to Him.

OUR FIRST PRIORITY

First of all, then, I urge that entreaties and prayers, petitions and thanksgivings, be made on behalf of all men, for kings and all who are in authority, so that we may lead a tranquil and quiet life in all godliness and dignity. (I Timothy 2:1–2)

Paul encouraged Timothy in regard to the priorities of the local church. He stated that "first of all" *prayer* be *the* priority of the church when it gathers together. I remember Dr. Stephen Olford relating to me the heartache he felt when in his travels he saw many churches omitting the pastoral prayer from their worship services. According to Scripture it is to be meaningfully done as a matter of first importance. It is to be a time that the church collectively gets under common burdens and does business with God!

In the same conversation, Dr. Olford related to me the story of being in a worship service under the leadership of Martyn Lloyd-Jones. He recalled the awesome experience of hearing Lloyd-Jones, the converted medical doctor whom God had called into the ministry, lead his congregation in prayer. The prayer lasted twenty-eight minutes! Although I am not encouraging any of us to follow this as a norm, the testimony was that in Lloyd-Jones's prayer, the whole congregation was drawn into God's presence. Prayer is to be of first importance in the priorities of the gathered church.

A KEY TO GOD'S WORK

Jesus was going through all the cities and villages, teaching in their synagogues and proclaiming the gospel of the kingdom, and healing every kind of disease and every kind of sickness. Seeing the people, He felt compassion for them, because they were distressed and dispirited like sheep without a shepherd. Then He said to His disciples, "The harvest is plentiful, but the workers are few. Therefore beseech the Lord of the harvest to send out workers into His harvest."
(Matthew 9:35–38)

When Jesus saw the needs of the multitude, He felt a deep compassion for them. He deeply felt their stress and troubled hearts as they were in desperate need of the care, love, and protection that only the Lord can give. In this moment of deep concern He spoke to His disciples. What did He say?

Jesus instructed His disciples to pray and "beseech the Lord of the harvest to send out workers into His harvest" (Matthew 9:38). Why did He do this? Did He desire His disciples to get a good feeling from prayer? Did He remind them not to miss their devotions for the day? No, He asked them to pray because He knew how heaven works! The usual method of God accomplishing His work is to place a prayer burden on someone's heart. That person responds to the prayer burden by praying. In Matthew 9:37 Jesus attempts to place the prayer burden on the disciples' hearts by helping them see and feel the need of the multitudes, and in 9:38 He encourages them to pray in response to this burden.

In prayer we can become co-laborers with the sovereign God of the universe. In the words of J. Oswald Sanders, prayer "invests puny men with a sort of omnipotence." When one grasps in the heart how God works, he can understand why Andrew Murray said, "We understand then that our true aim must not be to work much; and have prayer enough to keep the work right, but to pray much and then to work enough for the power and blessing obtained in prayer to find its way through us to men."

A KEY TO GREAT FRUITFULNESS

One pastor was overwhelmed with his counseling load. He decided to schedule his counseling appointments thirty minutes earlier than he planned to meet with the counselees. When they arrived he told them he would see them in thirty minutes and suggested they spend this time in the sanctuary talking to the Wonderful Counselor about their problem and asking for His wisdom and guidance. The pastor found that many no longer needed counsel after spending that half hour alone with God!

George McCluskey, whom we mentioned in chapter 17, realized that God works through prayer, and he carried the burden of his family to the Lord each day. God also desires you and me to commit to Him the prayer burdens that He entrusts to us.

James Dobson was asked one day why He believed God had given him the privilege of having such a prominent ministry at Focus on the Family. He humbly replied that the prominence had little to do with him, his dear wife, Shirley, or even their incredible staff. His first explanation was the prayer life of his father who seemed to live in the presence of God. Dr. Dobson said about his father:

> While praying early one morning in 1977, he was given the assurance that his own ministry would reach millions of people with the Gospel of Jesus Christ, although he would not live to see it. The Lord told him that it would be accomplished through me. My dad suffered a massive heart attack the next day from which he never recovered. What a humbling legacy that has been handed down from the soul of this great man.

God has chosen to work through prayer. S. D. Gordon said, "The greatest thing one can do for God and for men is to pray. You can do more than pray after you have prayed, but you cannot do more than pray until you have prayed. Prayer is striking the winning blow; and service is gathering up the result."

I give an assignment for students to write out in two to three pages the major influences that have shaped their lives. The opening paragraph of one of these papers said:

> I believe the single most influential event that caused me to be where I am spiritually was the life of my great great great grandfather. He was a circuit riding preacher in Missouri, Illinois and Kentucky. My grandmother tells me that he would pray that God would raise someone up to preach the gospel from his family. I am the only descendant of that man who entered the ministry. I believe that I am an answer to his prayers. I have his Bible, and I can read his notes. The thought that someone who prayed over 100 years ago for me influences me even today.

What prayer burdens has God put upon your heart? As you respond to these, you can be used to bestow countless blessings that may extend far beyond your own lifetime!

To be sure, the development of a prayer life is a spiritual battle, and this book will make every effort to help you in this battle. Corrie ten Boom stated, "The devil smiles when we make plans. He laughs when we get busy. But he trembles when we pray especially when we pray together." As Andrew Bonar puts it, "The Prince of the power of the air seems to bend all the force of his attack against the spirit of prayer."

Let us remember that no one becomes a marathon runner overnight. However, in your training be careful not to get discouraged and project your own attitude onto God. I remember Richard Foster saying that just because *you* do not think that your prayer life is important does not mean that *God* thinks it is not important. Another helpful thought from Foster is not to conform God's amazing prayer promise to your own impoverished experience, but rather to seek God and ask Him to shape your experience to His incredible promises.

One of the wisest requests you can make is "Lord, teach me to pray." As we learn from Jesus' response in Luke 11, God will never be indifferent to the one who earnestly makes this plea and is willing to do all that He suggests. Why not even ask God to enable you to get addicted to the joy of prayer? Remember that such a request is certainly in God's will, for "the prayer of the upright is His delight" (Proverbs 15:8).

In the fall of 1982 some godly men from several churches in our community decided to set aside five Saturday mornings to seek the Lord and be instructed from God's Word about the teaching of revival. The meeting was held about a mile from the apartment in which I lived at that time.

In my walk back to my apartment following the hours of prayer in one of these Saturday mornings, I passed a fine gospel-preaching church and it seemed God put this thought in my mind—"Would you like to have a ministry in this church?" Before I could even come up with a reply in my mind this thought entered it—"You can have a ministry in that church or in any church or in anybody's life if you will let Me teach you how to pray."

To be sure, both the Spirit of God and the Evil One can plant thoughts in our minds. Our thoughts can be influenced by other human factors as well. I believe these thoughts were the Spirit of God, and I believe they could apply to any believer. Why not cry out to the Lord, "Teach me to pray." We might not be able to speak in any pulpit we choose, but we certainly can pray for any pulpit. People may not be willing to listen to us, but they cannot stop us from praying for them. We can only be in one place at one time, but our prayers can cover more than one continent. What an awesome opportunity to realize that you can cooperate with God and lift the spirit of an individual half a world away from you. "Lord, teach us to pray."

The Help
of Fasting

This may be the key to your spiritual
breakthrough—this is what the Bible teaches.

Learning
When to Fast

And Jesus said to them, "The attendants
of the bridegroom cannot mourn as long
as the bridegroom is with them, can they?
But the days will come when the bridegroom
is taken away from them, and then they will fast."

≯ MATTHEW 9:15

After D. L. Moody's church was burned in the Chicago
fire, he went to England in 1872. The purpose of his
trip was not to preach but to study and to listen to others
preach while his new church was being built. After a prayer
meeting one night a London pastor, John Lessey, spotted
Moody and urged him to preach for him the next Sunday.
He was at first reluctant but finally agreed. In the morning
service, the audience seemed very indifferent. He confessed that it was the hardest time he had ever had preaching in his life. The thought of having to preach again that
night was quite discouraging, but he knew he needed to be
faithful to his promise.

The evening service was an entirely different atmosphere. Moody sensed the energizing presence of the Spirit

of God. In his words, "The power of an unseen world seemed to have fallen upon us." At the close of the sermon he asked those who desired to become Christians to please stand. All at once about five hundred people rose to their feet. Assuming there was some mistake he asked them to sit down, and then he repeated the invitation, and the same number arose from their seats. He asked them to again be seated and stated that all who desired to become Christians should step into the inquiry room. The entire group entered, and extra chairs had to be put into the room. In the inquiry room Moody once again asked them to stand, and the whole audience responded to the invitation. After he prayed for them and presented the Gospel, he asked for all of them who were really earnest to meet the pastor here the next night. More people came on Monday night than had been present on Sunday, Moody was urged to return, and he ministered for ten days!

Moody sensed that there was some unusual prayer behind this amazing response. He later found out that a bedridden girl name Marianne Adelard had heard about Moody's presence from her sister after he had preached in the morning. She had been praying for God to send revival to her congregation, and she had also read an article about D. L. Moody. She kept the article under her pillow and continually asked God to send this man to her church. When she learned he was there, she asked her sister to lock her door, send her no dinner, and refuse all visitors so that she could spend the afternoon and night in prayer and fasting. God was delighted to work in response to her prayer.

Marianne Adelard kept a birthday book in which people could sign their name next to the date of their birth. In that book G. Campbell Morgan, a London pastor, recalls seeing "D. L. Moody Psalm 91" beside February 5. On Moody's follow-up visit to her, she pledged to pray for him until she or he went home to be with the Lord.

WHAT IS FASTING?

Richard Foster defines fasting as the "voluntary denial of a normal function for an intense spiritual activity." In the Bible the reference is primarily to eating, but Scripture also mentions temporarily abstaining from the physical relationship in marriage (1 Corinthians 7:5) and from sleep (2 Samuel 12:16; Daniel 6:18).

In other words the Bible's emphasis is on fasting from food but it refers to a broader use of abstinence from other things. In some cases these things can knowingly or unknowingly become a substitute for God. Therefore, one might benefit from a media fast, or fasting from such things as recreational shopping. The purpose of all such abstinence in the words of Norwegian theologian O. Hallesby is "to loosen to some degree the ties which bind us to the world or material surroundings as a whole in order that we may concentrate all our spiritual powers upon the unseen and eternal things." The abstinence is not to be an end in itself but rather for the purpose of being separated to the Lord and to concentrate on godliness. This kind of fasting reduces the influence of our own self-will and invites the Holy Spirit to do a more intense work in us.

There is nothing meritorious in fasting in the sense that through it one earns something from God. Christ's death on the cross earned for us every spiritual blessing (Ephesians 1:3). Every spiritual discipline should rest on the foundation of Christ's finished work. However, fasting can be a discipline that seeks to experience the life of victory that Christ has purchased for us. When one fasts from food a greater amount of blood, usually needed for digestion, is available for mental and spiritual concentration. As Neil Anderson says, "Eating is the grand-daddy of all appetites. Fasting is a commitment to bring about self-denial and overcome every other conceivable temptation." It is a response to the Lord to seek Him and abstain from food or another normal activity to make your whole heart available to Him.

WHAT ARE THE KINDS OF FASTS?

In describing the types of fast our discussion will be limited to the Bible references to abstinence from food. A *normal fast* is to abstain from all food but not water. It is assumed by most Bible scholars that Jesus drank water during His forty-day fast. First, the reference in Matthew 4:2 refers to His hunger but not His thirst. Second, normally the body can only function three days without water.

An *absolute fast* is to abstain from all food and drink. Ezra ate no food and drank no water as he mourned over the unfaithfulness of God's people (Ezra 10:6). Esther requested a three-day absolute fast on her behalf as she sought God to deliver His people from destruction (Esther 4:16). After the apostle Paul was converted on the road to Damascus he experienced a three-day absolute fast (Acts 9:9). The record of Moses' (Deuteronomy 9:9) absolute fast of forty days is usually put into the category of a *supernatural fast.* An absolute fast of this duration clearly required God's supernatural intervention in order to sustain the body.

Daniel 10:3 refers to a three-week *partial fast,* in which Daniel abstained from "tasty food," meat, and wine. The emphasis of a partial fast is upon a restriction of diet rather than a total abstinence from all food.

WHEN DO I FAST?

It is accurate to say that Jesus does not command His followers to fast, but He certainly did *expect* fasting to be a part of their lives. Matthew 6 records His instructions about giving, praying, and fasting. The references to "when you give," "when you pray," and "when you fast" clearly show His expectation that these disciplines would be practiced by His people. In fact He plainly stated that after His departure from earth His followers "will fast" (Matthew 9:15).

Not only is fasting recorded in the book of Acts, but church historian Philip Schaff notes that throughout the first three centuries Christians fasted twice a week.[1] They did this with reference to the Lord's word in Matthew 9:15 and in remembrance of Jesus' suffering and death. The choice of Wednesday and Friday was to separate the Christian practice from the abuse of the regular Monday and Thursday fast of the Pharisees (Luke 18:12).

Should a believer fast on a regular basis? There are no commands in Scripture that require it. The only biblical pattern of a regular fast was on the Day of Atonement (Leviticus 16:29–30; cf. Psalm 35:13; Isaiah 58:5; Acts 27:9). At least four other annual fasts had been adopted by the Jewish people by the time of Zechariah (Zechariah 8:19), but there is no biblical command for them. A believer is spiritually free and perfectly accepted by God on the basis of Christ's work alone. But as Foster says, "Our freedom in the gospel, however, does not mean license, it means opportunity."[2] The apostle Paul's freedom led him to fast (Acts 14:23). Some of his fasting may have been involuntary due to his circumstance and suffering, but no doubt it was also to cultivate the enjoyment of the fellowship of the Bridegroom (Matthew 9:15). The ultimate answer to the question of regular fasting lies in the heart of God, which He is willing to disclose to each of His individual children. All fasting needs to be focused on the Lord, directed by Him, and empowered by Him.

Fasting has even been an important part in the history of nations. It was a part of the life of the pilgrims who came to America. They adopted the practice of setting aside special days to fast and pray, and even passed a law on November 11, 1636, that allowed the governor and his assistant to order days of fasting. When America was on the verge of a war with France, President John Adams commanded a fast on May 9, 1798. In 1815 James Madison issued a proclamation for the nation to fast. Abraham Lincoln, on three occasions in his administration, proclaimed a national fast. Even more relevant is the long list of godly men in the church who bore witness to the benefit of prayer and fasting. Martin Luther, John Wesley, George Whitefield, Jonathan Edwards, David Brainerd, Henry Martyn, Andrew Bonar, and Hudson Taylor are a few that could be mentioned. The greatest relevance to you is the answer to the question, "Lord, how do You desire *me* to make use of this discipline in my life?"

Experiencing the Benefits of Fasting

When I heard these words, I sat down and
wept and mourned for days; and I was fasting
and praying before the God of heaven.

❧NEHEMIAH 1:4

Bob Moeller tells an exciting story about a church that
faced major spiritual obstacles. Although he has
changed the names and place, it is a true story, and worth
quoting in full.

SMOG IN THE SANCTUARY

Even casual observers recognized signs that something was seriously wrong at Church of the Foothills
in eastern Texas. It had been through a series of short
pastorates. Some members of the congregation
sniped frequently at staff members, and their shots
often found the mark.

Once, in a crowded lobby, an angry parishioner up-
braided a staff member about an earlier meeting. On an-

other occasion, a choir director was verbally abused over his music selection. Sunday could be such a day of contention that some previous pastors had requested prayer just for strength to make it through the day.

When Pastor David Henson arrived, one woman asked him if he were aware of the history of the church. "When I tell my friends I go to Church of the Foothills," she told him, "they offer me sympathy."

New Pastor, Same Battle

Pastor Henson soon began receiving letters from individuals attacking his character and ministry. So biting and belligerent were the tone of some, he could scarcely believe Christians could say such things to a fellow believer. One man tore out the pastor's page from the annual report, scribbled caustic notes all over the page, and sent it back to him—anonymously. In the bottom corner of the page was an ominous comment: "You must go."

To Pastor Henson it seemed that a spiritual smog hung over the church. Then several people, independent of each other, told him how they felt despair and depression when they drove into the long church driveway. Henson experienced the same phenomenon. "One morning as I drove up the expressway, I looked over at our property," he says. "I could see a darkness hovering above our building. I don't want to go into that place, I thought. I want out of here."

His level of concern rose when his brother-in-law came to visit one Sunday. He phoned later and said, "David, I could sense a heaviness in the worship service."

"What do you mean?" Henson asked.

"I sensed something awful and unseen in the sanctuary," he said, "directly above the piano, organ, and pulpit."

"I've felt it too," Henson replied. "That's exactly where I've experienced it."

In the face of both a visible and invisible struggle, Pastor Henson concluded this was a case like that described by Jesus in Matthew: "This kind does not go out except by prayer and fasting." So he began to pray and fast. He even prayed out loud as he entered the church building or his office, though no one was around to hear him.

Henson had to work hard to keep his balance during this difficult time. His denominational tradition hardly acknowledged the reality of evil spirits, and he knew a fixation on demons was not the hallmark of a healthy ministry. But he felt compelled to confide in a few trusted friends and ask them to pray that the congregation be released from this dark hand of oppression.

During this time, Henson began receiving obscene calls on his voice mail. Hundreds of hang-ups harassed him. One voice mail call was a death threat. Henson notified the police. When the police listened to the recordings, the sergeant said, "I don't know who you're dealing with, but he's an intensely angry, volatile individual."

There were days when Henson was overwhelmed with a desire to resign and put the pain and pressure of the situation behind him. At times he would literally hold on to the edge of his desk to keep himself from getting up and walking out.

The angry threats were real, but were they part of a spiritual offensive aimed at driving him out and rendering Church of the Foothills spiritually inoperative? All Henson knew was that Satan's goal is to rob God of glory.

He sought the advice of several leaders outside the church. One church consultant had heard of the church's problems, so when he was working in the area, he decided to drive by the property. Later, he told Henson, "When I turned in the property, I was overwhelmed by a sense of the demonic." He stopped his car and sat there for almost ten minutes. When he finally left, he said to himself, "This place is a spiritual shell."

Two Events

Shortly after the consultant gave Henson his assessment, two significant events took place at Church of the Foothills.

The first came at the close of Henson's sermon series on prayer and fasting. He suggested that the people pray and fast in a spirit of repentance, asking God to lead them to restoration and accountability. A number of people stood to commit themselves to a ministry of prayer and fasting.

Not long after that response, the spiritual smog started to lift. Several individuals testified about conquering long-term habits. Then, almost a year later, a second change came: people began to leave the church, some for legitimate reasons, others not. At the same time, however, God seemed to open the door to outsiders. Numerous visitors appeared in the worship services.

But there was another profound change yet to take place: in Pastor Henson himself.

Through all the difficulties, he had felt so unloved that he found his affection for the people dampened. One day Henson left the church in a mood as dark and melancholy as the clouds that hovered outside. "I felt I had given it my best, but my best had not been good enough," he says. "I didn't think I could go on. It was as though I was knocked down in the final moments of a fifteen-round boxing match. I had no strength left to get up off the mat."

But as Henson drove home, he suddenly broke down and began to weep. He wept so hard he couldn't see the road and had to pull to the side of the expressway. He cried out to the Lord to forgive him for his lack of love for the church. He asked for the new heart of a shepherd. Just then, the sun broke through the clouds. Pastor Henson looked at the bright beams and said, "Lord, do that same thing in my heart."

New Pastor, New Church

Gradually, what had taken place in Henson's heart began to spread through the congregation. The Sunday worship atmosphere of formality and stiffness softened. The services began to be marked by a sense of the presence of the Lord Jesus Christ. Each Sunday a group began to gather early in the morning to pray for the worship service.

The harsh, discouraging notes Henson had formerly received were gradually replaced by positive and encouraging letters—eventually a five-inches-high stack that recounted the ways God was working.

One person wrote, "Thank you for your willingness to stand on God's Word regardless of the consequences. . . ." Another said, "You and the other leaders have provided the environment for us to move forward in power."

"I no longer fear opening my mail," says Henson.

Church of the Foothills, through prayer and fasting, found the strength to stand.

A great celebration occurred when they were asked to host a regional conference for representatives from more than two hundred churches. The conference concluded with a Friday night Communion service in the sanctuary. Henson sensed an overwhelming sense of the brightness of the Spirit of God that night—"the most powerful worship experience I had ever been involved in." He could scarcely believe that just a few years before, the building had groaned under the weight of oppression. Now it could be a place of joy and celebration of God.[1]

PHYSICAL BENEFITS OF FASTING

It is helpful to give your body rest. When you fast, the digestive system is able to rest, and your circulatory and nervous systems are able to slow down. Fasting aids the cleansing of the body as the body is able to concentrate on the elimination of toxins. This elimination tends to sharpen your senses.[2] However, physical reasons for fasting are definitely secondary to spiritual reasons.

SPIRITUAL BENEFITS OF FASTING

The aim is the cultivation of a conscious enjoyment of God's presence in one's life. This is clearly the spirit of Jesus' teaching in Matthew 9:15. John Piper maintains that "the absence of fasting is the measure of our contentment with the absence of Christ."[3]

If you desire true contentment and joy in God, you will find the discipline of fasting is helpful to strengthen the intensity of your prayer (Luke 2:37) and your repentance (Joel 2:12). Bill Bright elaborates on these spiritual benefits in his book *The Coming Revival: America's Call to Fast, Pray and Seek God's Face* by noting the following seven spiritual benefits:

1. Fasting is a primary means of restoration. By humbling us, fasting releases the Holy Spirit to do His revival work within us. This takes us deeper into the Christ-life and gives us a greater awareness of God's reality and presence in our lives.

2. Fasting reduces the power of self so that the Holy Spirit can do a more intense work within us.

3. Fasting helps to purify us spiritually.

4. Fasting increases our spiritual reception by quieting our minds and emotions.

5. Fasting brings a yieldedness, even a holy brokenness, resulting in an inner calm and self-control.

6. Fasting renews spiritual vision.

7. Fasting inspires determination to follow God's revealed plan for your life.[4]

One other spiritual benefit to note is the increased insight we can receive regarding the things that control us. As the apostle Paul stated, "All things are lawful for me, but not all things are profitable. All things are lawful for me, but I will not be mastered by anything" (I Corinthians 6:12). Not only can it aid us in identifying the destructive attitudes of fear, anger, jealousy, pride, and greed, but also the gifts of God that have gotten out of balance in our life. When you allow your appetites to become your *god* (cf. Philippians 3:19), you lose the ability to truly enjoy God's gracious gifts. Foster stated that "our human cravings and desires are like rivers that tend to over-flow their banks; fasting helps keep them in their proper channels."[5] All actions that are not prompted and empowered by the Spirit are dead works. Fasting can make us sensitive to efforts in our life that are done apart from Christ (John 15:5).

Getting Started

Blow a trumpet in Zion, consecrate a fast,
proclaim a solemn assembly, gather the people,
sanctify the congregation, assemble the elders,
gather the children and the nursing infants.
Let the bridegroom come out of his room
and the bride out of her bridal chamber.

⸎ JOEL 2:15–16

SPIRITUAL PREPARATION FOR FASTING

One needs to first be aware of the abuses of fasting.
Any attempt to earn God's blessing through fasting is
clearly in contradiction to the scriptural teaching that
Jesus' death and resurrection is the ground for every spiritual blessing. Fasting is a humble response that puts us in a
place to receive the life and victory Jesus has won for us.
Second, one should never view fasting as a substitute for
repentance and obedience. To do so turns fasting into a
form of penance (cf. Isaiah 58:1–11). A third abuse is to
use it to impress others. This is clearly what Jesus forbids
in Matthew 6:18. The question is not so much whether
others know about our fast but rather why we want them

to know about it. The Scriptures make reference to corporate fasts, and thus fasting is not always a private matter.[1]
A fourth abuse is to belittle the kind gifts of God. While
on one hand we can fall in love with the gift of food and
not the Giver, on the other hand we can fail to enjoy the
food with the taste buds that He provided and glory in
our will power.

It has already been stated that we should fast as God
directs and empowers us. We do not live under a command that prescribes how and when it is to be done by
every Christian. However, D. L. Moody used to say, "If
you say 'I will fast when God lays it on my heart,' you never
will. You are too cold and indifferent to take the yoke
upon you." The truth is that part of needed spiritual
preparation is to confess and repent of any fear of fasting.
I like Donald Whitney's suggestion to have a fast of dedication as an expression of one's willingness to fast as the
Holy Spirit would direct.

PHYSICAL PREPARATION FOR FASTING

It is always best to precede a fast with nutritional eating
habits and even repentance for a lack of this. In some cases,
a doctor's approval and guidelines might be necessary, such
as with an expectant mother, a heart patient, or a person
with diabetes. It may not be best to begin with an extended
fast. You can start with one meal or with a twenty-four-
hour fast when you eat the noon or night meal and do not
eat again until the following noon or night meal. A juice

fast may also be a profitable way to begin, abstaining from all food but drinking nutritious juice during the fast. One can even consider a partial fast from sugar. These are only suggestions as you will be guided by the Lord to achieve His purposes.

A PLAN AND PURPOSE FOR FASTING

When I was first exposed to the idea of this discipline many years ago, I sought to put it into practice. I really did not know what I was doing, and I am not sure how much was spiritually accomplished by my efforts. I fasted because I thought it was what I should do. What I lacked was a clear plan and a purpose. Lacking a God-focused purpose for fasting can be quite a self-centered experience. It should be done for the Lord (Zechariah 7:5) and motivated by love for Him and others (I Corinthians 13:1–3).

My experience changed when I entered a fast with a specific spiritual objective. I remember taking a day to fast for guidance in regard to the topic of a thesis I had to write. I had been writing down possible ideas during my year at seminary. On this day of fasting the decision became clear. I knew that I would be spending a lot of time in research and writing on this project. I chose the topic "Principles of Christian Living from Romans 5–8." The lessons learned in this project have been extremely helpful in my life and ministry. I've experienced the same grace in other times of looking for God's guidance. God honors any effort of setting aside time to seek Him.[2] In times of spiritual warfare, fasting can be a God-appointed means to experience Christ's deliverance (Matthew 17:21; Mark 9:29).[3] Fasting may be to express your intense concern for the work of God (Nehemiah 1:4) or even to express your grief (2 Samuel 1:11–12; 12:16, 21–23). To keep your desires under the control of the Spirit (cf. 1 Corinthians 9:24–27; Romans 13:14) is another legitimate purpose.

Are you in need of a spiritual breakthrough in your life or ministry? What is God laying upon your heart? Plan a time to seek God in fasting. Allow yourself time to get in the Scripture and time for extra rest if it is an extended fast. Be alert that you will need self-control on the other side of your completed fast. May God bless you abundantly as you seek Him. Remember that He is a wonderful, gracious God who delights in you beyond your highest imagination.

The Waiting
of Prayer

*Realizing what God is doing while you wait can
give you hope. Discover the benefits of waiting.*

23

Experiencing the Joy of Waiting

But the Lord answered and said to her,
"Martha, Martha, you are worried and
bothered about so many things; but only
one thing is necessary, for Mary has
chosen the good part, which shall
not be taken away from her."

⇣ Luke 10:41–42

Imagine being continually and cruelly rejected by your own people—your efforts to love them being met by both indifference and intense hatred. Ponder awakening each morning to the reality that there was a plot to kill you. One of your closest associates will betray you and deliver you up to be killed. Your most vocal supporter will deny even knowing you, and all your other close friends will desert you. Where would you go for support if you had no spouse, your own brothers misunderstood you and even mocked you, and your closest friends let you down in your hour of greatest need?

Suppose I told you that the person who actually experienced these stressful circumstances lived with continual peace and was the most joyous person who ever lived (Hebrews 1:9). This person, of course, is Jesus Christ, and He desires to share with you His peace (John 14:27) and His joy (John 15:11) as you learn to wait before Him.

- How would like to learn to live triumphantly above fear and anxiety?
- How would you like to learn to truly enjoy life?
- How would you like to be free to experience and express true love and to triumph over being critical and judgmental?

The secrets of these blessings unfold as one learns to wait on God. The truth of "waiting" is found throughout the Bible. We can observe the following descriptions of waiting on the Lord:

- wait continually (Hosea 12:6)
- wait silently (Lamentations 3:26; Psalm 62:1, 5)
- wait patiently (Psalm 40:1)
- wait eagerly (Isaiah 26:8)

The following inspired account of a simple event that happened hundreds of years ago still has great relevance to your life today.

Now as they were traveling along, He entered a village; and a woman named Martha welcomed Him into her home. She had a sister called

> *Mary, who was seated at the Lord's feet, listening to His word. But Martha was distracted with all her preparations; and she came up to Him and said, "Lord, do You not care that my sister has left me to do all the serving alone? Then tell her to help me." But the Lord answered and said to her, "Martha, Martha, you are worried and bothered about so many things; but only one thing is necessary, for Mary has chosen the good part, which shall not be taken away from her."* (Luke 10:38–42)

In a brief but profound story God gives us the record of a lady who found joy in waiting on Christ. The story might be called "The Tale of Two Sisters." One of the sisters welcomed Jesus into her home. However, she did not enjoy the visit and experienced great stress during His stay. The other sister, on the exact same occasion, experienced great delight in the Lord's fellowship. She portrayed a life of "waiting" on Christ.

Why does Jesus rebuke Martha and commend Mary? A superficial look at Luke 10:38–42 leads to the wrong conclusion that Jesus rebuked Martha for her diligent service. The rebuke was not for her service but rather for the attitude that characterized her service. In her service she was "distracted," "worried," and "bothered." It was not service itself that Christ rebuked but the anxiety and restlessness surrounding it.

In all fairness to Martha, it is important to state that the more responsible you feel for the "success" of a ministry endeavor, the greater the temptation to worry and be anxious about it. After all, it was she who welcomed the

Lord into her home. The Lord's rebuke reveals His care and love for us in our frazzled state. The Lord loves and accepts His children at all times, but He loves us so much that He has not sentenced us to serve Him with an anxious heart and distracted mind. The Lord wants to train us to enjoy Him in all of our endeavors, no matter how small or how big.

The Lord desired to deliver Martha from the evil and bitter fruit of her attitude in her "service." When we exercise our wills before we exercise our faith, our service leads to doubt, dissatisfaction, and a critical attitude—"Lord, do You not care that my sister has left me to do all the serving alone?" The greatest crime is the "demanding spirit" that drives this kind of service as revealed in Martha's words, "Then tell her to help me." The evil is not only doubting the Lord's care but also forgetting the truth of who we are—Christ's servant, not His master.

Mary was commended not because she was idle while Martha worked. Actually Mary was "waiting" on the Lord as she listened to His word. Her life is an illustration of what it means to abide in the Lord. She was listening to Him and willing to do anything He desired. Waiting does not necessarily mean inactivity, but it does mean a life of obedient faith.

The section of Scripture that preceded Jesus' visit to Martha and Mary is the story of the Good Samaritan (Luke 10:25–37). The Lord's instruction about prayer is what follows (Luke 11:1–13). The surrounding accounts are not chronologically related, but their inspired placement is related thematically. Why did the Spirit of God lead Luke to sandwich Jesus' rebuke of Martha and commendation of Mary between the bookends of spontaneous compassion and prayer? The "hurried" and "anxious" spirit of Martha not only chokes and quenches the Spirit-led compassion that the Good Samaritan illustrated, but it also is the death of true prayer. The spirit of Mary who chose the "good part" opens one up to see the needs of others and cooperate with God in His loving plan. This waiting on the Lord is also the attitude of prayer.

Jesus commended Mary because her abiding in the Lord and waiting on Him is the only way to live a life of eternal significance. Jesus said the good part that she chose "shall not be taken away from her." As we abide in the Lord we can do an eternal work even in the midst of the routine of life. We are able to accomplish *nothing* of eternal value apart from the enablement of Christ (John 15:5).

The benefits of "waiting" are quite numerous. These are some that the Bible mentions:

- Freedom from shame (Psalm 25:3)
- Courage (Psalm 27:14)
- Strength (Isaiah 40:31)
- God's promises (Psalm 37:9)
- Deliverance from the bitter fruit of self-effort (Psalm 106:13–15; Isaiah 30:15–18)
- Vindication (Proverbs 20:22)

- God's favor (Psalm 147:11)
- God's salvation (Lamentations 3:26)
- God's support (Isaiah 64:4)

The next chapters will give practical guidance about how God develops a heart that waits on Him.

24

Discovering God's Purposes While You Wait

But I am afraid that, as the serpent deceived
Eve by his craftiness, your minds will be
led astray from the simplicity and
purity of devotion to Christ.

≥ 2 CORINTHIANS 11:3

John was a fellow college student I was discipling more than thirty years ago. As a new believer he was facing one of the greatest crises of his life—his mother was very ill, and he was petitioning God to spare her life. After pouring out his heart in prayer, he was in anguish when the result was not in line with his request. She died.

Tom was a roommate in college and a very gifted person. One day in an unusual moment of candor he told me why he had very little interest in the Lord. He said it all went back to a childhood experience. He was smaller than the other boys who were his age but full of determination and eager to prove himself on the football field. In a special needy moment in one football game he called on God to help him. He said that it just did not work. The Goliaths on the field continually manhandled him. He wondered, *Why should I be interested in a God who disappointed me?*

Dorothy came to me and told me about her girlfriend who had all of a sudden developed a whole new mind-set about the Lord. Her enthusiastic service had been transformed into cynical skepticism. Dorothy was in hope that I, as her professor, could help her answer the long list of intellectual questions that her girlfriend had. I responded by asking one question, "Has your girlfriend gone through a deep disappointment?" Dorothy told me that she had gone through a breakup with her boyfriend. I knew that this was her real question, and, in this case, the intellectual questions were only a mask to disguise her bitterness toward God.

Does not God say, "Ask *whatever* you wish, and it will be done for you" (John 15:7, italics added)? Does He give a blank check that can be cashed with our desires? But what about John, Tom, and Dorothy's friend? If one is to learn to wait on God in prayer, he needs to be mindful of five things.

IN PRAYER GOD IS SEEKING TO GET US UNDER HIS LOVING AUTHORITY

We are to come to God as His servant and not as His master. The true essence of prayer is found in the Lord's words in Gethsemane, "Yet not what I will, but what You will" (Mark 14:36). If one prays to God in a spirit that refuses to listen to God's Word, the prayer is said to be an abomination (Proverbs 28:9).

What does James mean when he writes, "You ask and do not receive, because you ask with wrong motives, so that you may spend it on your pleasures" (James 4:3)? He certainly does not mean that if you really desire something you cannot pray for it. However, it does mean that when your desires are the lord of your life and you desire their fulfillment more than you desire God, your prayers will be hindered. James's admonition to these believers is to "submit therefore to God" (James 4:7).

What does it mean to "submit to God"? It means that we are willing to submit our desire to Him, knowing that His will is exactly what we would desire if we knew all the facts. It does not mean pretending that we do not have desires. Even the Lord Himself prayed "remove this cup from Me" before He prayed "yet not what I will, but what You will" (Mark 14:36). People under God's authority are free to talk to God about their concerns, their fears, and their anger. God invites us to pour out our hearts before Him (Psalm 62:8)! Our desires are based on our knowledge and perception, which are always limited—but our trust is in the omniscient God who loves us.

Submitting to God means that we are willing to make any adjustment in our lives that God desires. Prayer is not attempting to get our will done in heaven but His will done on earth. A number of years ago I read a book that criticized the use of the phrase "if it be Thy will" as the ending to our prayers. The author's point was that it is too often an expression of our unbelief. It is our way of saying, "Lord, I don't think You are going to do anything, and just so You don't look bad, I will say 'if it be Your will.' The author is correct in saying that it should not be used this way, and that Scripture in many cases tells us what is God's will. For example, you can petition God with confidence to be a vessel of love to your spouse, to forgive one who has hurt you, and to live above bitterness. However, Paul did pray to come to Rome "by the will of God" (Romans 1:10; 15:32). In some cases all we know is that we have a persistent desire and we continue to submit it to the Lord. Paul continually lifted up His desire to go to Rome. When he did travel to Rome he came "in the fullness of the blessing of Christ" (Romans 15:29) but not as he expected. He came as a prisoner, but this was acceptable to one who was willing to make any adjustment in his life to fulfill God's will.

Submitting to God means that we are willing to be involved in the answer to our prayer. Being involved in the answer involves obedient faith. It is not the same as scheming in our own self-effort as Abraham did with Hagar (Genesis 16:3). It is offering yourself up to God after you have prayed to be used in any way that He would desire in order to fulfill His will.

IN PRAYER GOD IS SEEKING TO GET US DEPENDENT ON THE SPIRIT

I have previously written about praying in the Holy Spirit (in section 2). A few quotes will suffice to make our point here. God does not desire prayer to be a mere formality or an empty ritual with no expectation.

"Is there not much praying in which there is no prayer?" (Samuel Chadwick)

"Very often when we cry to God we do not really mean anything." (D. L. Moody)

"It is delusion of the devil to think that we cannot pray; we can if we really want anything. It is not the most beautiful or eloquent language that brings down the answer, it is the cry that goes out of a burdened heart. It is the desire, the wish of the heart, that God delights to answer. An arrow if it be drawn up but a little way, goes not far, but if it be pulled up to the head, flies swiftly and pierces deep. Thus prayer if it be only dribbled forth from careless lips, falls at our spirit. Fervency of spirit is that which availeth most." (D. L. Moody quoting Bishop Hall)

IN PRAYER GOD IS SEEKING TO GET US WALKING IN THE LIGHT

The following scriptural insights may help as you wait upon the Lord.

- Is there an idol in my life—someone or something other than God that I look to to meet the thirsts and desires of my heart? (Ezekiel 14:3)

- Is there willful sin in my life about which I have not openly and honestly talked to God? (Psalm 66:18)

- Is there a persistent sin of omission in my life that God has brought to my attention? (Proverbs 28:9; James 4:17)

- Is my attitude in my relationships pleasing to God? (Matthew 5:23–24; I Peter 3:7)

- Is there anyone in my life that I am not willing to forgive? (Mark 11:25)

IN PRAYER GOD IS SEEKING TO DEVELOP A LOVE MOTIVATION

Are my prayers motivated out of a critical spirit? Are my prayers motivated only by my own self-interest? Paul's compassionate desire for his Jewish people led him to express his Christlike love in prayer (Romans 9:1–5; 10:1). As Christ had become our curse that we would be delivered from hell, Paul wished that it were possible to do the same for the people who had greatly persecuted him.

IN PRAYER GOD IS SEEKING TO TEACH US TO LIVE FOR HIS GLORY

"Not to us, O Lord, not to us, but to Your name give glory because of Your lovingkindness, because of Your truth" (Psalm 115:1).

Christ died to deliver us from only living for ourselves

(2 Corinthians 5:14–15). His love is designed to win your heart to Him and show you the goodness of His name. Man seeks to glorify his own name at the expense of others. God glorified His name by coming to earth as a man and dying for His enemies. In our prayer we are not to seek to draw attention to ourselves (Matthew 6:5) but rather to the Lord and the accomplishment of His kind and loving purpose. This led Jonathan to pray for David's welfare and kingship rather than seek his own selfish ambition of succeeding his father Saul. Take your prayer burden and petition to the Lord to honor His glorious character.

A great emphasis in prayer is what God desires to do in us. He desires to get us under His loving authority, dependent on His Spirit, walking in the Light, motivated by His love, and living for His glory. The collective essence of these five truths is an abandonment of one's life to the Lord and a continual openness, dependence, and responsiveness to His loving control. As Dr. Bill Bright once said, "If all your desire is the glory of God and the well-being of others it is impossible to ask God for too much." God patiently seeks to do this in us as we wait on Him.

25

Transforming Your Anxiety into Peace

*But though I am always in haste, I am
never in a hurry, because I never
undertake any more work than I can go
through with perfect calmness of spirit.*

&JOHN WESLEY

The student body was shocked and delighted when
Dr. George Sweeting came to the pulpit after the
morning chapel had concluded and announced that the
following day's classes would be cancelled. He had been
deeply moved by the message and announced that classes
would meet, but only for prayer.

In a single announcement God had freed my schedule
for the next day by relieving me of all my teaching responsibilities. I began to think, *How can I make use of this day?
Should I fast?* It did not appear that God was impressed with
any of my ideas. In the midst of this extremely busy fall,
God simply wanted to slow me down and rejuvenate a tired
body. I ate a good breakfast that morning and boarded the
commuter train to Chicago to experience one of the most
unusual days of my life.

On this day I sensed a great need to put down all my normal disciplines and be quiet before the Lord. I even spoke as few words as possible as I guided my classes in corporate prayers. At the end of the day I walked to the train and returned to my apartment. If you had seen me and inquired, "What did you do today?" I could have only replied, "Nothing but be still and quiet."

Before I boarded the train I went into a restaurant to get a meal. I was single at this time and a regular customer at a couple of restaurants. (They probably thought I died when I got married.) On this occasion a waitress said something that had never been said to me previously. She said it not once or twice but three times. She said, "I go all over this restaurant and I sense hurry and rush, but I come to your booth and I sense peace." I believe God wanted to knock me over the head and show me the fruitfulness of following His leading. It was as if He said, "If I ever lead you to slow down—even from your efforts of seeking and serving Me—I want you to know that it pays great spiritual dividends."

HOW ANXIETY HINDERS GOD'S BEST

As we learn to wait on the Lord, we need to learn to live at His pace.

Unless the Lord builds the house, they labor in vain who build it; unless the Lord guards the city, the watchman keeps awake in vain. It is vain for you to rise up early, to retire late, to eat the bread of painful labors; for He gives to His beloved even in his sleep. (Psalm 127:1–2)

God's pace is not the same as the hurried spirit of the world. John Wesley, the early Methodist leader who is known for his godly diligence, stated, "Leisure and I have taken leave of one another."[1] I did not know what to do with that statement and still do not, because there seems to be a legitimate place for leisure. It was a later statement that made a greater impression upon me. Wesley said, "But though I am always in haste, I am never in a hurry, because I never undertake any more work than I can go through with perfect calmness of spirit."[2] This diligent man had learned to live at God's pace.

Moving to Chicago in 1980 was an exciting adventure as I walked through the door of opportunity that God had graciously opened to teach at the Moody Bible Institute. As a twenty-eight-year-old professor I walked into a class that students thought was to be taught by a seasoned veteran teacher who had left to go to another ministry. One student sat on the back row and shook his head in disagreement at almost every assertion I made as I taught the Prison Epistles.

As a result, when I came to lecture on Philippians 4:6–7 I had a special thirst for this topic of God's peace and the Lord's wonderful command to be "anxious for nothing." I diligently searched the Scriptures to seek to understand what the Lord was saying. To experience God's peace does not mean a life free from all difficulties and opposition. After all, Philippians 4:6–7 was not first spoken from a pulpit, but rather written from a prison. The Lord Himself told His followers that they would have tribulations in this world, but in the midst of this they could experience His peace (John 16:33).

God's peace does not mean a freedom from all emotion and concern. The apostle Paul wrote about being concerned about the things of the Lord (1 Corinthians 7:32), being concerned for one's spouse (1 Corinthians 7:33), and being concerned for God's people (1 Corinthians 12:25; 2 Corinthians 11:28). Peter spoke of being "distressed" by trials in the midst of rejoicing (1 Peter 1:6). True peace does not demand a denial of our emotions and concerns. What is the difference between godly concern and sinful anxiety? Actually the same Greek word is used for both, and it is only the context that reveals the difference. The difference can be seen in these mathematical formulas.

Concern + unbelief = anxiety.

Concern + faith = a biblical virtue.

God desires us to carry our concerns in an attitude of faith. God desires to aid us in casting our cares upon the Lord (1 Peter 5:7).

As I prepared for this lecture more than twenty-five years ago I listened attentively to God's Word. Going to this class was always stressful because of one very bitter student who sought to be disruptive. As I traced the uses of the Greek word translated "anxiety," I discovered four reasons that God wanted me to experience His peace.

1. *Anxiety accomplishes nothing positive* (Matthew 6:27). Someone has said that worry is like a rocking chair—it gives you something to do but gets you nowhere. I am reminded of an old poem about a cow: "The worried cow would have lived now if she had saved her breath; but she feared her hay wouldn't last all day, so she mooed herself to death."

2. *Anxiety chokes God's Word from bearing fruit* (Mark 4:19). One can digest and assimilate God's Word only in an atmosphere of inner peace. Those who teach God's Word need to be attentive in aiding others to cast their cares upon the Lord. There may be a spiritual reason that Sunday morning can be a very anxiety-filled time as one prepares to worship with other believers.

   There may be times that you are listening to someone but not able to hear what the person is saying because of the anxiety racing around your mind. As I was counseling someone one day I was very distracted. I said, "I really want to listen to you but I have a very heavy heart. Would you please take just a moment and pray with me as I seek to give my concern to the Lord?" He gladly agreed, and after our prayer I was able to listen attentively to him. As he began to talk he started weeping and began to tell me what he really wanted to tell me.

3. *Anxiety hinders our perspective* (Luke 21:34). Jesus tells us that some will not be prepared for His coming because they will be weighed down with the ordinary concerns of life. Even the routines of life can weigh one down with anxiety, and certainly a special crisis can do so. Thoughts about one's family, finances, job, and health can turn to anxiety and cloud our perspective. Interpersonal relationships can be some of the greatest worries as we fret over something we did, or said, or something done or said to us.

4. *Anxiety steals opportunities* (Luke 10:38–42). Anxiety stole the opportunity for Martha to enjoy fellowship with her Lord. Sin is a thief that can "withhold good from us" (see Jeremiah 5:25). Anxiety can steal the good of fellowship with the Lord as one seeks to serve Him.

HOW TO EXPERIENCE GOD'S PEACE

Let your greatest concern be living under God's rule and in harmony with His truth (Matthew 6:33).

This is the way Jesus concluded His sermon on how to live above anxiety. One common ingredient to worry is assuming responsibility that God never intended us to have. We certainly can be anxious over another person's response to us, the results of a ministry or business endeavor, or the future of a child. What we have to discern is the answer to this question, "What is my responsibility in the matter?" We can take full responsibility of being a vessel of love to another and can pray for a desired response, but we cannot take full responsibility for the responses of others.

A dear man of God came up to me and discussed his heavy heart about an important relationship in his life. He said that every time he was around a certain older man he walked away feeling guilty because the man appeared to never be pleased with him. I responded, "If you take responsibility for this man's response to you, then this man can determine whether or not you have a good day." In this sense God wants us to be "free from all men" (I Corinthians 9:19) in order to love others as we seek His rule over our life and attempt to live in harmony with His righteous ways (Matthew 6:33). If our anxiety is due to our sin (cf. Psalm 38:18), then we need to confess it and be cleansed and returned to a right relationship with God.

There is no peace for the wicked, according to Isaiah 57:21. This verse may seem far away from you, but let me ask you one question, "What is more wicked than telling the Lord that He cannot rule over an area of your life?" Seeking His kingdom first of all means seeking to personally live under the rule of King Jesus.

Learn to live one day at a time (Matthew 6:34).

Mark Twain observed, "I am an old man and I have seen a lot of troubles, but most of them never happened."

God only gives grace to live one day at a time. Although this does not mean one should not plan for tomorrow, it does mean that we are to fully live today, and any future planning that needs to be done will be done in the context of living for today. C. S. Lewis said that "the present is the only time in which any duty may be done or grace received."

I spoke one night a number of years ago to a singles group. After the meeting a man in his thirties came up to me with a Bible and his finger on a verse. He said, "What does this verse say?" The verse was in Proverbs 5, which gives the command to the married man to rejoice in the wife of his youth (v. 18). He told me that he was getting old—not a youth—and his wife was not here! Anything I said to him only made him angrier even though I also was single at that time. Finally, I asked him, "Do you think that you can make it through the rest of the day as a single man?" "Oh, yes," he replied. "That is all the faith you will ever hope to have," I told him. This truth calmed down the very angry person. We can face anything by trusting God one moment at a time. We will get anxious after we envision our problems or concerns in the days, weeks, months, and years ahead. Each day God will faithfully supply new merciful help (Lamentations 3:22–23).

Learn to unburden your heart (Philippians 4:6–7).

Every temptation to be anxious is a call to prayer. We must also petition and supplicate God. The Scriptures can aid us in learning how to do this with our various concerns. There are times it has been helpful for me to write out my prayer and document the Scripture I am studying. This process is a help when we are tempted to take back the care that we have cast upon the Lord. When this happens we can rehearse to the Lord how we have committed the concern to Him. Thanksgiving is the final key part of the process in Philippians 4:6. If we do not mix our prayers and petitions with thanksgiving, we will get more wrapped up in the problem than in the Lord.

Seek the aid of others (Galatians 6:2).

God is the One who bears our burdens, but He will often choose to work through others. There are times that the counsel, encouragement, and prayers of trusted friends is a necessary part of the process. In certain cases it is good to bring a matter to the elders or leadership of the church. God gives grace as we humble ourselves before others.

Now may the Lord of peace Himself continually grant you peace in every circumstance. The Lord be with you all! (2 Thessalonians 3:16)

26

Knowing When
to Keep Praying

Behold, as the eyes of servants look to
the hand of their master, as the eyes of
a maid to the hand of her mistress, so
our eyes look to the Lord our
God, until He is gracious to us.

ᴪ PSALM 123:2

George Mueller had prayed for the salvation of two
men for more than fifty years when someone asked
him, "Do you think God is going to save those men?" He
replied, "I certainly do, for God would have never kept
them on my heart for fifty years if He did not intend to
do so." One was saved shortly before Mueller's death and
the other shortly afterward. As Raymond Edman said, "It
is always too soon to quit."

A lady came to Jesus one day and began to cry out to
Him saying, "Have mercy on me, Lord, Son of David; my
daughter is cruelly demon-possessed" (Matthew 15:22).
The shocking thing is the Lord's response. Jesus seemingly
ignored her and "did not answer her a word" (Matthew
15:23). The Canaanite lady continued to shout for help

from the disciples, and their only response was to say to Jesus, "Send her away, because she keeps shouting at us" (Matthew 15:23).

The Lord's response seems to be very uncharitable. Can you think of times that you have cried out to God and felt ignored by Him? Have you ever felt like He has not given you any response to your plea? Have you ever felt like your cries were even a burden to the Lord's people, and they viewed you only as a bother and a nuisance? If so, you may be learning some special lessons about waiting on the Lord. But hang in there, for it might get worse before it gets better!

The Canaanite lady continued to pursue the Lord. She fell at His feet to worship Him and cried out, "Lord, help me!" (Matthew 15:25). The first time He appeared to ignore her. This time He seems to be a little hard on her by replying, "It is not good to take the children's bread and throw it to the dogs" (Matthew 15:26). If someone first ignores your cry for help and then appears to clearly reject it, you usually get the message that it simply is not worth pursuing the matter any further. However, the Canaanite lady was different. She kept persisting in conversing with the Lord, "Yes, Lord; but even the dogs feed on the crumbs which fall from their masters' table" (Matthew 15:27).

How did Jesus respond to this persistent faith? He not only granted her initial request—the healing of her daughter—but He even gave her *more*. She received one of the four compliments of Jesus that are recorded in the Bible.

"O woman, your faith is great; it shall be done for you as you wish" (v. 28). This compliment of the Lord undoubtedly transformed her life. Christ's response of seemingly ignoring her and appearing to be hard on her was to elicit a perseverance in prayer to give her not only what she asked for but even more than she knew how to ask.[1]

Christ desired not only to reward her for one act of loving faith but to transform her by His compliment into a lady of faith. One Christian leader recalls a boyhood experience of talking to a friend about the Lord. His father responded, "You are a little soul winner." He thought that he did not deserve this compliment since the boy did not respond to the gospel, but it planted in his mind a vision for what he aspired to be.

The greatest influence of how you view yourself is your perception of how the most important person in your life views you. A girl in a godly Christian home seemed to continually rebel against her father. In his great concern for her he had repeatedly exclaimed, "You are going to become just like your wrong friends." Without realizing it the father gave her a vision of failure and rebellion that she fulfilled. As we wait on the Lord, He can become the most important person in our life, and His loving input can uproot the thoughts that are not in harmony with His truth.

Warren Wiersbe has stated that perseverance in prayer is not overcoming God's reluctance but rather laying hold of God's willingness. Our sovereign God has purposed to sometimes require persevering prayer as the means to accomplish His will. I say "sometimes" because there are occasions when we pray once for a matter, and the prayer is answered immediately.

WHY HAS GOD CHOSEN TO WORK THROUGH PERSEVERING PRAYER?

- To purify our desires. Sometimes we may want the right thing for the wrong reasons. Why do we desire our church to grow—to honor God and benefit souls or to make us appear successful? Why do we desire our child to behave and do well—for the honor of God and the child's spiritual well-being or for our reputation as a parent? God entrusts us with concerns in order for us to learn to persevere and pray. And as we do, He does a work in us.

- To prepare us for His answer. A premature answer might cause us to glory more in the gift than in the Giver. As we persevere in prayer our hearts are being prepared to truly enjoy the gift in a way that will enhance our fellowship with God.

- To develop our life and character. We have already stated that one of God's greatest priorities in prayer is the work He desires to do in us. We noted in chapter 24 how He desires to use our prayer to get us under His loving authority, dependent on His Spirit, walking in the light, motivated by love, and living for His glory.

- To be used of God in spiritual warfare. Although we are not told a great bit of detail about the exact nature of the angelic conflict in the heavenlies, we are told enough to be assured of the reality of it. The "delay" in the answer to Daniel's prayer was due to this angelic conflict (Daniel 10:12–13).

• To bless us with a more intimate relationship with God. An aspect of delighting in a person is delighting in conversing with them. The joy of fellowship with a prized person is the greatest treasure. This is certainly true in our relationship with God. The gift of Himself is His greatest gift to us (Romans 8:32).

WHAT DOES SCRIPTURE SAY ABOUT PERSEVERANCE?

• Direct instruction from Scripture to persevere

Isaiah 62:6–7—Look at the phrase, "You who remind the Lord, take no rest for yourselves; and give Him no rest."

Matthew 7:7–11—Prayer is the only subject mentioned twice in the Sermon on the Mount. The present tense imperatives of Matthew 7:7 carry the sense of "keep on asking," "keep on seeking," and "keep on knocking."

• Parables of Christ that encourage persevering prayer

Luke 11:5–8—The response of an unwilling friend to perseverance should encourage the believer to persevere to our heavenly Father who is good and generous.

Luke 18:1–8—The response of the unrighteous judge to the widow's plea encourages the believer to cry out in faith to a righteous Judge.

• Examples of God rewarding perseverance

Genesis 18:22–33—God heard Abraham's intercession for Sodom; though Sodom itself was destroyed, Lot was rescued.

Genesis 32:24–29—God honored Jacob's persevering in prayer for God's blessing and protection from Esau.

WHEN SHOULD YOU PERSEVERE IN PRAYER?

When you desire God more than you desire the answer to your prayer. You can see that it is a strong desire that undergirds persevering prayer. The stern rebukes of the multitude could not quiet the cries for mercy from the blind Bartimaeus. He was able to clearly articulate his desires to God, and Jesus compassionately answered his request (Mark 10:46–52).

The psalmist prayed to the sovereign God of the universe and saw himself as His *servant* (Psalm 123:1–2). The psalmist declared that he would persist in prayer until he received God's gracious answer.

We can persevere with this strong desire as long as our posture is that we are God's servant and He is not our servant. There is a difference between a fleshly stubbornness and a godly perseverance. The former insists on getting one's will done in heaven, and the latter determines to get God's will done on earth. Paul submitted his strong desire to the Lord for the removal of the "thorn in the flesh." In his perseverance he was also open to hear the Lord's guidance that his request was not in line with God's will (2 Corinthians 12:7–10).

When you are standing on the Word of God. The *clearest* way to know you are praying in the will of God is to pray Scripture to the Lord as we stated in section 4. Certainly you can know with absolute certainty that it is God's will to answer the prayers that are in line with Scripture. Start out by believing God to answer Philippians 1:9–11 each day in your life. You can also stand on God's Word knowing that it is His will to give you the grace to carry out any scriptural vows you have made to the Lord—such as marriage vows.

When you are willing to wait on God's timing for the answer. An unwillingness to wait may reflect a lack of submission in your life. As you commit your request to the Lord you can rest in the joy that it is not forgotten by God. The beautiful words of Solomon's prayer are assuring to the child of God who is patiently persevering in prayer.

> *And may these words of mine, with which I have made supplication before the Lord, be near to the Lord our God day and night, that He may maintain the cause of His servant and the cause of His people Israel, as each day requires, so that all the peoples of the earth may know that the Lord is God; there is no one else.* (1 Kings 8:59–60)

A persevering intercessor is characterized by the ability to see and internalize how God desires to bless. He or she is also an advocate for the ones who stand in need of this blessing. The most telling characteristic is that the person continues to pursue the matter in prayer until it is received. John Hyde, later known as praying Hyde, received an unusual letter one day. The letter stated, "I'm going to pray for you until you are filled with the Spirit." This intercessor sensed a prayer burden from the Lord to pray for this servant of God in the early part of John's missionary career. He pursued this matter, and the rest is history as John Hyde was eventually empowered by God's Spirit in his prayers and service for the people of India.

As I have sought to study the prayers of Scripture, I have discovered these "aids to persevering intercession." Why not right now take the burden that is in your heart and use these as you pray to God?

- Appeal to God's attributes (Psalm 51:1).

- Appeal to God's promises (Genesis 32:9–12).

- Appeal to God's honor or reputation (Exodus 32:12; Psalm 25:11; Psalm 115:1).

- Appeal to the need of God's people (Exodus 14:10; Psalm 86:1).

- Appeal to God's past action (Psalm 4:1).

- Appeal to our union with Christ (Romans 15:30).

- Appeal to the truth that God may be known (Exodus 33:13).

Ask God for the grace of intercession, and He will enable you to keep appealing to Him until the issue has been answered or resolved.

SECTION

9

The Power of Praise

There are precise reasons that God says worship and praise is mandatory for your spiritual health—here is why, what praise is, and how to develop a life of praise.

27

Experiencing the
Goodness of Praise

Praise the Lord! For it is good to
sing praises to our God; for it is
pleasant and praise is becoming.

꒾PSALM 147:1

In the early days of David Wilkerson's work among the gangs in New York City, a group of boys was walking toward him as he neared a street corner. As he approached these boys there were clear signs that they were planning to attack him. Taking his fear to the Lord and praying for guidance, Wilkerson continued to advance toward the gang. In the moment that they appeared poised to strike him, he clapped his hands and without any warning shouted, "Praise the Lord!" Wilkerson reported that the entire gang immediately fled. Billheimer in his book *Destined for the Throne* attempts to give the reason for the behavior of the gang. He believes that the most plausible explanation is that the boys who were activated by evil spirits panicked at the shout of genuine praise.

Praise is declared to be "good" in Psalm 92:1 and

147:1. The same God who demonstrated His glory by coming to the earth as a baby and later dying for His enemies is the One who commands His people to worship Him (Matthew 4:10). The loving heart of God that was so clearly revealed on the cross is the motivation behind His seeking worshipers (John 4:23).

Although worship and praise is an *end* in itself and not a means to an end, it does result in countless benefits. This is because we are worshiping a good God. Worship is the primary thing, and it is God's way that when one focuses on the primary thing one will get the secondary things. For example, when one seeks first God's kingdom and His righteousness, this is the pathway of obtaining the provisions we need to do God's will (Matthew 6:33). In a similar vein, delighting in the Lord is the way to experience the deep desire of one's heart (Psalm 37:4).

WORSHIP LEADS TO THE TRANSFORMATION OF LIFE

It is a law of God that a person becomes like the one he focuses on. For many years I placed 2 Corinthians 3:18 at the top of my prayer list. As a person beholds or focuses on God's glorious character, he is transformed into His image. For example, as we uphold His loving patience and absolute faithfulness, His Spirit works this fruit in our life. On the other hand a person who beholds an idol loses spiritual vitality. Observe these verses from Psalm 115:

Their idols are silver and gold,
The work of man's hands.
They have mouths, but they cannot speak;
They have eyes, but they cannot see;
They have ears, but they cannot hear;
They have noses, but they cannot smell;
They have hands, but they cannot feel;
They have feet, but they cannot walk;
They cannot make a sound with their throat.
Those who make them will become like them,
Everyone who trusts in them. (Psalm 115:4–8,
emphasis added)

WORSHIP ENHANCES MENTAL, EMOTIONAL, AND SPIRITUAL HEALTH

Worship delivers a person from the lie that there is
someone or something other than God who is worthy of
our ultimate trust, affection, and adoration. In the heart
of every person is a conscious or unconscious search for
this object of worship. Worship and praise declares the
search to be over and overcomes this deceit.

King Nebuchadnezzar was disciplined by the Lord
and lost his mental health. In a mental illness known as
zoanthropy and observed in modern time, one thinks of
himself as an animal and acts like one. This may have been
the diagnosis of the king. What is clear is that his *reason re-*
turned to him when he raised his eyes toward heaven and
"blessed the Most High and praised and honored Him
who lives forever" (Daniel 4:34). In this way the proud

man became a humble man. Praise and worship is the cure for pride and the pathway to spiritual health.

WORSHIP ENHANCES
HUMAN RELATIONSHIPS

Worship gives purpose and meaning to relationships since the deepest fellowship with others is found in inviting them to worship the Lord with us. "O magnify the Lord with me, and let us exalt His name together" (Psalm 34:3).

In this sense true worship demands reconciliation with others we have offended (Matthew 5:23–24) so that "with one accord you may with one voice glorify the God and Father of our Lord Jesus Christ" (Romans 15:6).

WORSHIP STRENGTHENS FAITH

"Without faith it is impossible to please [God]" (Hebrews 11:6). It is logical that if we are occupied with the object of our faith in praise and worship, our faith will be strengthened. The admonition is that the only object worthy of boasting is not wealth, power, or wisdom but rather understanding and knowing God (Jeremiah 9:23–24).

WORSHIP LEADS TO THE
EXPERIENCE OF GOD'S PRESENCE

God declares Himself to be enthroned upon the praise of His people (Psalm 22:3). It is for this reason that C. S. Lewis wrote, "It is in the process of being worshipped that God communicates His presence to man."[1]

The manifested presence of God is not to be equated with the omnipresence of God. Although God is everywhere, He is not manifested everywhere. In the Old Testament era God manifested Himself in the tabernacle and in the temple. Today He manifests Himself in His church. The greatest compliment one could ever give a church is to come into the assembly and fall on his face, worship God, and declare, "God is certainly among you" (I Corinthians 14:25). When God's Spirit is grieved by sin and quenched by disobedience, this presence is not manifested. Just as God disciplined Israel in the Old Testament by letting His glory depart (Hosea 5:6; Ezekiel 10), so He disciplines His church by withdrawing His manifest presence. It can be restored by repentant worship (Psalm 51:16–17).

WORSHIP GIVES PERSPECTIVE

The continued testimony of Scripture is that the only way to deal with trials is to place them in perspective.

For I consider that the sufferings of this present time are not worthy to be compared with the glory that is to be revealed to us. (Romans 8:18)

For momentary, light affliction is producing for us an eternal weight of glory far beyond all comparison, while we look not at the things which are seen, but at the things which are not seen; for the things which are seen are temporal, but the things which are not seen are eternal. (2 Corinthians 4:17–18)

In this you greatly rejoice, even though now for a little while, if necessary, you have been distressed by various trials, so that the proof of your faith, being more precious than gold which is perishable, even though tested by fire, may be found to result in praise and glory and honor at the revelation of Jesus Christ. (1 Peter 1:6–7)

When Asaph struggled with his trials in comparison to the comfortable lives of the godless, he was troubled until he found perspective. This perspective did not come until he went "into the sanctuary of God" (Psalm 73:17). In worship we can be drawn to God and see His eternal perspective.

Ronald Allen and Gordon Borror also give another aspect of how worship gives perspective.

The story is told of a craftsman who had traveled to America from Europe to dedicate his life to some of the detail work of one of his country's grandest places of worship. One day a sightseer was touring the edifice and observed the workman meticulously laboring near the high ceiling on a symbol which could hardly be seen from the floor. What is more, he seemed to be occupied with a detail on the top, even out of view of the most carefully observant worshipper. The sightseer said, "Why are you being so exact; no one can see the detail you are creating from the distance?" The busy artist replied, not missing a stroke, "God can!"[2]

WISDOM LEADS TO GUIDANCE AND SERVICE

It was as the church was "ministering to the Lord and fasting" that the Spirit of God gave guidance to set apart Barnabas and Saul for a missionary trip (Acts 13:2). As Isaiah was occupied in worship to God he also received the Lord's commission (Isaiah 6). It is for this reason that Jesus declared that the Lord alone is to be *worshiped* and *served* (Matthew 4:10), for we will serve the one we worship.

WORSHIP LEADS TO SPIRITUAL VICTORIES

I was deeply troubled when I observed a student's lack of integrity as she appeared to be cheating on an exam. After calling the student into my office I confronted her concerning her behavior. Looking me straight in the eye, the student calmly denied that she had cheated. I accepted her word and told her that I was delighted to be wrong. All was well until I observed the same thing *again.*

What was I to do? I had already confronted the person. And she seemed to have the ability to deny it and maybe even convince herself that she was not guilty. My heart was heavy because I did not know how to help keep her from a pattern of deceit that could lead to great devastation.

The thought of this dilemma often greatly discouraged me. I received counsel from one who told me what to do every time I entertained this discouraging thought. A friend told me to use the occasion to praise Jesus Christ every time I was discouraged over the matter. It was the dose of medicine that I needed! Satan so hates the genuine praise of Christ that his fiery darts of discouragement are not effective against us when we respond in *praise*. I not only found relief, but God also later sent another faculty member to me who had observed the same pattern in the student. He came to me without any solicitation on my part. When we both confronted her, the student responded and admitted her guilt!

If you were perfect in every way, the greatest gift you could give somebody would be to allow him to enjoy you for who you are. God in His perfection gives to us this great *gift*, and with it come countless other benefits.

Understanding
the Meaning
of True Worship

Worship is the submission of
all of our nature to God.

࣒WILLIAM TEMPLE

I ra Sankey, D. L. Moody's soloist, was traveling by
steamboat when he was asked to sing for the passen-
gers. When he finished singing the song "Savior, Like a
Shepherd Lead Us," a passenger came up and asked
Sankey if he had served in the Union army. Upon being
told yes, the man further questioned, "Can you remember
if you were doing picket duty on a bright, moonlit night
in 1862?" Again Sankey answered yes.

The man then explained that he had been in the Con-
federate army, and had seen Sankey and raised his gun to
shoot him when Sankey raised his eyes toward heaven and
began singing the same song he had just sung. He told
Sankey, "'Let him sing his song,' I said to myself. 'I can
shoot him afterwards.'" But when Sankey finished the
song, the soldier found himself unable to shoot. Now, he

told Sankey as he told him the story, he needed to find the cure for his sick soul. Sankey threw his arms around the man and told him about the Good Shepherd.[1]

Oswald Chambers in his classic devotional, *My Utmost for His Highest,* declared the worship of God to be the essential requirement for the spiritual fitness of every Christian. He even asserts that a person who is not a worshiper will be ultimately useless in his service and even a hindrance to others. In a classic interview with Eugene Peterson that was published by *Leadership* magazine in the spring of 1997, Peterson said that the most important thing a pastor does is guiding his people in worship. When this ceases to be the most important priority of his energy and imagination, he is no longer functioning as a pastor.

If worship is so important and carries with it so many benefits, we need to understand precisely what it is.

WORSHIP IS ASCRIBING
GLORY TO GOD'S CHARACTER

Worship comes from an Anglo-Saxon word meaning "worthship." The simplest way to define worship is that it is to attribute worth to God's revealed character. The command to "ascribe to the Lord the glory due to His name" in Psalm 29:2 does not mean we add anything to God. It simply means that we acknowledge Him for who He is and in this way glorify or honor Him. This is precisely what is being done in heaven, as we see in two passages that quote heaven's citizens:

Worthy are You, our Lord and our God, to receive glory and honor and power; for You created all things, and because of Your will they existed, and were created. (Revelation 4:11)

Worthy is the Lamb that was slain to receive power and riches and wisdom and might and honor and glory and blessing. (Revelation 5:12)

May God give the grace to do it on earth as we declare our amazement, awe, admiration, fascination, and confidence in God's beautiful character.

WORSHIP INVOLVES THE TOTAL PERSON

William Temple's definition of worship is often quoted, as it is helpful in underscoring this facet of worship: "Worship is the submission of all of our nature to God. It is the quickening of conscience by His holiness; the nourishment of mind with His truth; the purification of the imagination by His beauty; the opening of the heart to His love; the surrender of will to His purpose."[2]

Jesus declared that the greatest commandment was to love the Lord and that this love was to spring from our *total* person (Matthew 22:37–39). The problem with the worship of the Pharisees was that they honored God with their lips but their hearts were far from Him (Matthew 15:8). As evidenced by the first three uses of *heart* in the Bible, the "heart" is the control center of our inner person and involves our mind (Genesis 6:5), emotion (Genesis

6:6), and will (Genesis 8:21). For that reason when the psalmist addresses himself to bless or praise God, he appeals to "all that is within [him]" (Psalm 103:1).

"The eyes of the Lord move to and fro throughout the earth that He may strongly support those whose heart is completely His" (2 Chronicles 16:9). Why not ask God to make your heart completely His, to "unite your heart" to fear His name (Psalm 86:11)? God is lovingly seeking worshipers, and although none of us can offer a life that has never sinned, we can offer Him our whole heart.

WORSHIP INVOLVES A FAITH RESPONSE TO GOD'S CHARACTER

Henry Blackaby said in a form letter, "Genuine worship is when a person chooses to come into the presence of God and there is an encounter with God; when God literally so makes Himself known that there is an automatic response to the very nature of God. If a person can come into worship and go out the same man he come in, whatever he did, he didn't worship." Several things are underscored in Scripture about this faith response.

It is to be a conviction of your soul. Notice the resolve of David in these verses.

- *My heart is steadfast, O God, my heart is steadfast; I will sing, yes, I will sing praises!* (Psalm 57:7)

- *Every day I will bless You, and I will praise Your name forever and ever.* (Psalm 145:2)

It is to be a continual attitude that invades all of life.

- *I will bless the Lord at all times; His praise shall continually be in my mouth.* (Psalm 34:1)

- *Though the fig tree should not blossom and there be no fruit on the vines, though the yield of the olive should fail and the fields produce no food, though the flock should be cut off from the fold and there be no cattle in the stalls, yet I will exult in the Lord, I will rejoice in the God of my salvation.* (Habakkuk 3:17–18)

- *Whether, then, you eat or drink or whatever you do, do all to the glory of God.* (1 Corinthians 10:31)

- *In everything give thanks; for this is God's will for you in Christ Jesus.* (1 Thessalonians 5:18)

It is a response that involves an offering.

- Of ourselves (Romans 12:1–2)
- Of our substance (Philippians 4:16)
- Of our praise (Hebrews 13:15)
- Of our service (Hebrews 13:15–16)

With these elements in mind it is possible to identify unacceptable worship. It is unacceptable to worship any other god, because this is not ascribing to the One and only God the glory that is due Him (Isaiah 48:11). Idolatry is the result of rejecting the true God (Romans 1:21), who has revealed Himself to all through His creation.

Worshiping idols is not only forbidden (Exodus 34:14) but will be judged (Isaiah 2:6–11). When one worships God he must worship Him in response to the *truth* of His revelation.

Unacceptable worship is also when one attempts to worship with less than a whole heart. This is why ritualistic worship that does not spring from a surrendered life is called vain worship (Matthew 15:8–9; 23:23–28; Isaiah 1:15; Hosea 6:4–7; Amos 5:21–27; Malachi 1:6–14; 3:13–15).

Unacceptable worship is also not characterized by a faith response. When one attempts to worship God in his own self-will, the results can be quite costly. Self-will worship can be seen in the lives of Nadab and Abihu (Leviticus 10:1–11); Saul (1 Samuel 15:23); and Uzzah (2 Samuel 6:1–9). True worship always involves a response of complete dependence and obedience to God in our attitude and action.

If you are asking, "How can I cultivate a lifestyle of worship?" you are asking the most important question that can be asked. There has never been a person who asked this with sincerity, sought God for the answer, and purposed to do anything God would suggest who did not get the answer. The next chapter will explore this theme.

Abiding in
the Lord

I have held many things in my hands
and I have lost them all, but whatever
I placed in God's hands, that I still possess.

𝔰·MARTIN LUTHER

It was more than thirty years ago at Auburn University that I wandered into the room of a fraternity brother, but I did not realize that the encounter that day would ultimately completely change my life forever. Buster began to tell me about the person and work of the Holy Spirit. I did not ask any question or even utter a comment, but I hung on every word. I left the room with the thought, *Maybe there is hope for living the Christian life.*

At this time I had completed one year of college. I had made the Dean's list, been inducted into a very good social fraternity, selected to an honorary society, and elected president of the School of Business. Outwardly things were great, but inwardly I was bankrupt. Fear and anxiety characterized my inner world, although I had trusted Christ as my Savior.

In December Buster shared with me about the Holy

Spirit. I went home for the Christmas vacation with the objective of learning more about how the Spirit enables a believer to live the Christian life. I learned some things cognitively over the Christmas holidays, but it was in rooming with Buster for the next year that I saw the truth fleshed out in a life.

The key to unceasing prayer and worship is an abandonment of one's life to the Lord and a continual abiding in Him. What does this mean? When a person becomes a Christian, the Holy Spirit permanently indwells his life (cf. Romans 8:9), but that doesn't mean He always has full control. Dr. Stephen Olford explained the human responsibility in regard to appropriating the filling or control of the Spirit using the words *Open, Dependent,* and *Responsive.*

FILLING INVOLVES AN OPENNESS TO HIS CONTROL

Is there any area of your life that is not open to the Lord? Fear can be at the root of this rebellion of trying to control an area of life. As you open up your life to the Spirit's control, you do not get more of the Spirit, but He gets more of you. Years ago a church was deciding whom to ask to be the speaker of a special series of meetings. A member of the committee exclaimed, "Let's ask D. L. Moody." Another objected and said, "D. L. Moody does not have a monopoly of the Holy Spirit." "No, he does not," was the reply, "but the Holy Spirit has a monopoly on him."

IT INVOLVES A DEPENDENCE
UPON HIS CONTROL

This is where the freedom lies. Is there any concern or task that you are trying to work out on your own? Follow the simple admonition of Psalm 37:5, "Commit your way to the Lord, trust also in Him, and He will do it."

I often need to ask myself, "Is there any responsibility that I am engaging in that I have not first committed to Him?" You cannot trust God for something that has not been surrendered to Him. As you do trust Him, He will never make you irresponsible. However, be cautious not to try to do His responsibility.

One day I was writing a delicate letter to someone in an attempt to smooth over a misunderstanding. As I wrote I could feel tension all over my back. What I became aware of was that I was *depending on my letter* to resolve the misunderstanding. I put my pen down and told the Lord that I wanted to depend on Him alone to solve the problem. After the prayer I sensed His prompting to write the letter—but in peace. Dependence on the Spirit does not mean inactivity, but it does mean activating our faith before we activate our wills.

Hannah Whitall Smith related the following illustration to underscore this point.

I was once trying to explain to a physician who had charge of a large hospital the necessity and meaning of consecration, but he seemed unable to understand. At t I said to him, "Suppose in going your rounds among your patients, you should meet with one man who entreated you earnestly to take his case under your special care in order to cure him, but who should at the same time refuse to tell you all his symptoms, to take all your prescribed remedies, and should say to you, 'I am quite willing to follow your directions as to certain things, because they commend themselves to my mind as good, but in other matters I prefer judging for myself, and following my own directions.' What would you do in such a case?" I asked. "Do!" he replied with indignation—"Do! I would soon leave such a man as that to his own care. For, of course," he added, "I could do nothing for him unless he would put his whole case into my hands without any reserves, and would obey my directions implicitly." "It is necessary then," I said, "for doctors to be obeyed if they are to have any chance to cure their patient?" "Implicitly obeyed!" was his emphatic reply. "And that is consecration," I continued. "God must have the whole case put into His hands without any reserves, and His directions must be implicitly followed."[1]

IT INVOLVES A RESPONSIVENESS TO HIS CONTROL

Responding to the control of the Spirit involves keeping our obedience up-to-date. Is there anything God is prompting you to do that you are not doing? It involves confessing your sin so that there is no disagreement between your soul and God. "We are to be as sensitive to sin as the pupils of our eyes are to foreign matter," was Dr. Olford's admonition to me. Such is good advice.

It is only the Spirit who produces genuine worship and thanksgiving. Notice how the admonition to be filled with the Spirit in Ephesians 5:18 is followed by the results of "singing and making melody with your heart to the Lord" in verse 19 and "always giving thanks for all things" in verse 20. Worship is a human response to a divine initiative. A worshipful lifestyle is one that seeks, in Richard Foster's words, to "still human initiated activity" and live in obedience to God's promptings.

As we live before the Lord, unceasing prayer and worship involves sharing our heart with the Lord. It is turning our temptations into conversations with God. Such is practicing the presence of God.

As you walk openly, honestly, and transparently before God, then and only then will prayer and worship become a dynamic reality in your life. Walking openly and honestly is not to be equated with absence of struggle. It is rather taking our struggles into the presence of God. It is responding to the loving discipline of God. Zacharias was disciplined for his unbelief in response to the promise of God. This led to the temporary loss of his ability to speak (Luke 1:20). The first words he uttered when he regained his speech were praise to God (v. 64). As we respond to the discipline of God we experience the compassion of God given to the one who confesses and forsakes his sin (Proverbs 28:13). To everyone who seeks to walk uprightly, "praise is becoming" (Psalm 33:1).

A complementary truth to the filling of the Spirit is living under the control of Scripture. The Spirit's control is described in similar ways in Ephesians and Colossians.

> *Speaking to one another in psalms and hymns and spiritual songs, singing and making melody with your heart to the Lord; always giving thanks for all things in the name of our Lord Jesus Christ to God, even the Father; and be subject to one another in the fear of Christ.* (Ephesians 5:19–21)

> *Let the word of Christ richly dwell within you, with all wisdom teaching and admonishing one another with psalms and hymns and spiritual songs, singing with thankfulness in your hearts to God.* (Colossians 3:16)

It is God's Word that explains to us how to be open, dependent, and responsive to God's Spirit. Although there is a subjective side of the Christian life, without God's Word one loses an objective standard. God's Word is the fuel that keeps the fire of prayer and worship burning in the soul of the person yielded to the Lord.[2]

Cultivating a
Lifestyle of Worship

Prayer is the natural and joyous breathing
of the spiritual life by which the heavenly
atmosphere is inhaled and then exhaled in prayer.

᳝ ANDREW MURRAY

After we made our first budget as a married couple my
wife burst into tears. She simply did not see how
there would ever be any money for many things she sensed
would be a blessing to our marriage and future family. She
did exclaim some years later that one of her greatest joys
has been experiencing God's gracious provisions to meet
our needs. We have kept a "Jehovah-Jireh" list on which we
have attempted to document God's provisions. (Jehovah-
Jireh means "The Lord will Provide.") Let me encourage
you to do the same. As God works through others to supply your needs, the result is not only the meeting of the
practical needs, but thanksgiving and praise to God
(2 Corinthians 9:12). I will close the book with five suggestions.

PUT ALL YOUR DREAMS AND DESIRES IN GOD'S HAND AND WAIT ON HIS TIMING

Simeon had received a promise that he would not die until he had seen the Messiah (Luke 2:26). All his life he waited on God to fulfill this word to him. One day this righteous man entered the temple to worship God. On that same day Mary and Joseph brought the baby Jesus to the temple, and Simeon broke out in praise to God for the fulfillment of God's word to the world and to him personally (vv. 29–32). One who waits on God to fulfill His plan and promises in His timing and in His way will live a life of praise.

REALIZE THAT ALL YOU HAVE IS DUE TO GOD'S GRACE

If I were getting what I deserve today, where would I be? You are correct; I would be in a place of eternal agony with no hope of any relief—and so would you. Our sins have earned this from God. Anything I ever receive in life other than God's judgment is due to His grace.

For years I have kept a daily journal of God's gracious blessing day by day. Every good and perfect gift comes from God according to James 1:17. Every smile, kindness, mouthful of food, refreshing rest, and any other blessing ultimately finds its source in God.

The world teaches us to live with the expectation that we deserve this or that. These may be conscious or unconscious expectations, but they destroy a spirit of thanksgiving and praise and open us up to bitterness. Take time to list the people in your family and ask God for what you can praise Him concerning each person. You can view any relationship in terms of what the person is not giving you (from the viewpoint of your expectations) or in terms of what he is giving (from the viewpoint of God's grace). Take another day to do this with your friends, associates, and pastors. Communicate to them the items for which you have thanked God. I have seen this simple exercise greatly benefit many people and their relationships, but most of all it brings pleasure to God.

I recommend you take a day and meditate on Ephesians 5:20, "always giving thanks for all things in the name of our Lord Jesus Christ to God, even the Father." I remember reading about a man of God who did this, and while brushing his teeth began to thank God for his toothbrush. Then he thanked Him for the toothpaste. He then realized that he had never thanked God for his teeth! We are forever indebted to the grace of God for every blessing.

REALIZE THE SPIRITUAL RICHES THAT YOU HAVE IN CHRIST

A number of years ago I divided my prayer life into different emphases for each day of the week. *Monday* was missionaries, *Wednesday*—Christian workers, *Thursday*—tasks I was involved in, *Friday*—family, *Saturday*—saints or fellow believers, and *Sunday*—sinners who needed to know the grace of God that could save them from their sins. On *Tuesday* I focused exclusively on thanksgiving and praise. One thing that really helped this emphasis was to go through Scriptures that note the spiritual blessings that God has given us. I would praise God for the blessings listed in Ephesians 1:3–14; Romans 5:1–11; Romans 6:1–23; and Romans 8:1–31. I have encouraged thousands of other people during the last twenty-plus years to do the same, and many have testified to the great profit of it.

REALIZE GOD'S SOVEREIGNTY AND GOODNESS IN YOUR TRIALS AND PAIN

D. Helen Roseveare was a missionary doctor in the Congo who was shamefully mistreated at the hands of some rebel soldiers. To try to make any sense out of her humiliation and suffering only seemed to awaken fresh pain in her heart. She finally got a great peace one day after she sensed God asking her, "Helen, are you willing to give thanks for that which I may never give you the privilege of understanding?"

God is sovereign and good and able to work together for good that which is not good in itself. He will and can put His healing hand on your hurting heart as you exercise your will and as an expression of faith choose to thank Him for trials that you do not yet fully understand. In so doing you honor the God who is ultimately the "Blessed Controller" of all of your life.

REALIZE THAT WORSHIP
IS A SPIRITUAL BATTLE

Worship and praise have great consequence, so do not get discouraged if you experience spiritual opposition. "Greater is He who is in you than he who is in the world" (I John 4:4). Trust God's wisdom, strength, and love as you seek to make prayer and praise your greatest priority.

A. W. Tozer wrote of the death of Brother Lawrence, a dear servant of God, who died many years ago in Europe. On his deathbed and rapidly losing his strength Brother Lawrence said to those who had gathered around him, "I am not dying. I am just doing what I have been doing for the past forty years, and doing what I expect to be doing for all eternity!" "What is that?" he was asked. He replied quickly, "I am worshipping the God I love!"[1]

May God bless you above and beyond your highest imagination as you cry out to God to build in you a praying heart that lives to worship God!

Personal Journal

Chapter 1

Write down specific fears and anxiety that can provide motivation for you to pray.

Talk to the Lord about the "Isaac" in your life.

Chapter 2

Write down one area of your life in which you feel inadequate and unworthy.

Review what it means to pray in Jesus' name, and pray in His name about the concerns you just recorded.

Chapter 3

Review Jim's testimony of God's response to his honesty in prayer.

Is there any hurt, pain, or temptation that you have for which you need to come boldly to the throne of grace and receive His mercy and grace?

Ponder Nathan's rebuke to David and use it as a motivation to tell your deepest desires to the Lord rather than going to the wrong well to have your needs met.

Chapter 4

Can you list past times of apparent defeat in your life that were precursors to special spiritual opportunities?

Ask God to give you a specific prayer burden to pray every time you encounter your most persistent temptation. Write down this prayer burden.

Consider forming a spiritual partnership with someone where you agree to pray for each other every time you are tempted.

SECTION TWO

Chapter 5

Has your prayer life ever "died" so that you have no expectancy in prayer?

Will you ask God to give you the grace of fervency and compassion that only the Holy Spirit can provide?

Review John Hyde's victory over his critical attitude in prayer. Trust the Spirit to give you His motivation in carrying whatever burden tempts you to be critical.

Chapter 6

What is the Spirit of God empowering you to believe God for today?

Chapter 7

Ask God how He desires to aid you in being sensitive to the Spirit's leading in your life.

Prepare for the next Lord's Day by writing down the three greatest concerns of your heart and sharing these with the Lord.

At this moment seek to get in touch with your heart and pray your concerns to the Lord.

Chapter 8

Is there some longing in your heart that is not being answered?

Could it be because God is desiring to grant you an even deeper longing and desire of your heart?

SECTION THREE

Chapter 9

What concern do you need to share with others to help you bear this burden in prayer?

Chapter 10

Is God prompting you to come to the elders and request prayer?

SECTION FOUR

Chapter 11

Look at Mueller's life purpose and ask God to give you one

that will clearly honor Him. If you know what it is, write it down to document it.

Ask God to give you a supernatural thirst for His Scriptures.

What obstacles hinder your finding time to get in God's Word?

Look at the promises God gives to one who meditates on Scripture, and believe God to overcome the obstacles you listed.

Chapter 12

Write down what it means to meditate on Scripture.

Chapter 13

Pray the three requests that we gleaned from Luke 2:40 for a loved one.

Ask God to encourage you by using Psalm 86:4–5 in your prayer.

Chapter 14

In light of the greatest concern on your heart, use Ephesians 1:15–23; 3:14–21; Philippians 1:9–11; and Colossians 1:9–12 to petition God.

SECTION FIVE

Chapter 15

Describe your struggle with the discipline of prayer. How does it compare with Baxter's struggle?

Chapter 16

Write down the four patterns of prayer in Jesus' life, and ask the Lord what application and guidance it gives to you.

SECTION SIX

Chapter 17

True or False   To take time to pray and put it into service is a bad investment.

True or False   To take time out of service and put it into prayer is a way to reap an enormous gain.

Discuss these questions with the Lord and ask Him to give you a conviction about the answers.

Chapter 18

Do you see God as "good" toward you?

The first step is to realize that you have earned His wrath. In His goodness Christ has earned our every spiritual blessing. It is up to you to humble yourself before God and ask God to show you His goodness and grace.

Chapter 19

Ask God to teach your heart the importance of prayer.

Write down the prayer burdens He has laid on your heart.

Remember that prayer begins with God, and He will give you the grace to pray the burdens that He puts on your heart as you humble yourself before Him.

Section Seven

Chapter 20

Ask the Lord how He desires you to use the discipline of fasting.

Chapter 21

Note the physical and spiritual benefits of fasting.

Chapter 22

Note the four abuses of fasting in your spiritual preparation.

Plan a fast of dedication to express your willingness to fast as the Holy Spirit would direct you.

What spiritual purpose is God giving you to motivate a fast?

Section Eight

Chapter 23

Write down your understanding of the different attitudes in Mary and Martha.

Chapter 24

As you share your greatest concern with the Lord, review the four purposes in this chapter.

Chapter 25

Review the four fruits of anxiety.

Seek to cast all your cares upon the Lord as you review the four truths relating to experiencing God's peace.

Chapter 26

What prayer burden has God given you with which to persevere?

What benefits have you experienced as you have persevered in prayer?

Evaluate your request by the three truths under the heading, "When should we persevere in prayer?"

SECTION NINE

Chapter 27

Evaluate your own worship by the benefits of true worship in this chapter.

Chapter 28

Evaluate your own worship by the description of true worship in this chapter.

Chapter 29

Are you abiding in the Lord? At this moment are you open to the Lord's control? At this moment are you depending on His control? At this moment is your life characterized by a responsiveness to His control?

Chapter 30

Take a day to meditate on the truth of Ephesians 5:20: "Always giving thanks for all things in the name of our Lord Jesus Christ to God, even the Father."

Take time to go through Romans 5:1–11; 6:1–23; 8:1–39; and Ephesians 1:3–14 and praise God for the blessings you have in Christ.

In a current trial, take time to worship God for His sovereignty and goodness.

Appendix I: Selected Prayers from Scripture

SELECTED OLD TESTAMENT PRAYERS
INTERCESSION FOR OTHERS
Genesis 18:22–33
Exodus 32:7–14, 30–34
Exodus 33:11–23 (also personal intercession)
Numbers 14:1–19 (prayer in 13–19)
Deuteronomy 9:7–29 (prayer in 25–29)
2 Samuel 7:18–29
Prayers for Guidance
Genesis 24:12–14
Judges 6:11–40

PRAISE AND THANKSGIVING
Exodus 15:1–18
Deuteronomy 32:1–43
Judges 5
1 Samuel 2:1–10
2 Samuel 22
1 Chronicles 29:10–20 (praise and petition)
Isaiah 25:1–8
Habakkuk 3

PRAYERS

For Protection and Blessing	Genesis 32:9–12; 48:15–16
	I Chronicles 4:10
	2 Chronicles 20:9
For Insight After Defeat	Joshua 7:6–15
For Miraculous Help	Joshua 10:12–14
For Blessing and Provision	Ruth 2:12; 4:14
For Blessing of Children	I Samuel 1:9–17, 20
For Commitment to a Friendship	I Samuel 20:12–23
For Confession and Repentance	2 Samuel 24:10–25
	Ezra 9
	Nehemiah 1:4–11; 9:5–38
	Job 42:2–6
	Lamentations 1–4
	Daniel 9:3–19
	Jonah 3
For Wisdom	I Kings 3:4–15
For Dedication	I Kings 8:22–9:9
For Vindication of God	I Kings 18:16–39
For Deliverance and Restoration	Genesis 20:17
	Exodus 2:23
	2 Kings 19 (cf. Isaiah 37:14–20)
	Isaiah 63:15–64:12
	Jeremiah 32:17–44
	Lamentations 5
	Amos 7:1–9
	Jonah 2
For Recovery from Illness	2 Kings 20:1–11 (prayer in verses 2–3)

WRONG ATTITUDE IN PRAYER

Jonah 4:1–10

Malachi 1:2, 6–7

SPONTANEOUS PRAYER
Nehemiah 2:4

PRAYER AND ACTION
Nehemiah 4:9

GUIDANCE TO NOT PRAY
Jeremiah 14:10–12

SELECTED PRAYERS FROM THE PSALMS
PRAISE AND THANKSGIVING (18, 21, 30, 32, 36, 40, 41, 66, 106,
　　　135, 138)

CONFESSION
(38, 51, 102, 130, 143)

IMPRECATORY (asking for God's justice on one's enemies)
(7, 35, 55, 58, 59, 69, 79, 109, 137, 139)

PETITIONS
For Guidance (Psalm 25:4–5; 31:3)
For Protection (Psalm 17:8)
For Encouragement (Psalm 86:4–5)
For Forgiveness (Psalm 25:7, 11)
For Self-examination (Psalm 139:23–24)

(Study the Psalms with an aim of finding Scriptures that help you
appropriately express your praise, confessions, and petitions to
God.)

SELECTED PRAYERS FROM THE GOSPELS
PRAYERS OF JESUS
Matthew 11:25–26
Matthew 27:46
Mark 14:32–40

Luke 22:31–32
Luke 23:34, 46
John 11:41–42
John 12:27–28
John 14:16
John 17:1–26

References to Prayer in Jesus' Life

Mark 1:35
Mark 6:46
Mark 10:13–16
Mark 14:22–23
Luke 3:21
Luke 6:12–13
Luke 9:18, 28–29
Luke 24:30–31, 50–51
John 6:11

References to Prayer Teaching of Jesus

Matthew 5:44
Matthew 6:5–15
Matthew 7:7–11
Matthew 9:38
Matthew 18:19–20
Mark 9:29
Mark 11:17, 22–26
Mark 13:33
Mark 12:40
Luke 6:46
Luke 11:5–13
Luke 18:1–14
John 4:23–24
John 14:12–14
John 15:7, 16
John 16:23–27

OTHER REFERENCES TO PRAYER IN THE GOSPELS
Luke 1:10, 13, 46–55, 64, 67–79
Luke 2:29–32, 37–38
Luke 23:42
Luke 24:52–53

REFERENCES TO PRAYER IN THE BOOK OF ACTS

1:13–14, 24–25
2:21, 42
3:1, 8
4:24–31
6:4, 6
7:59–60
8:14–17, 22–24
9:5–11, 40
10:1–8, 9–16, 30
11:5
12:5, 12
13:2–3
14:23
16:13, 16, 25
20:32, 36
21:5
22:16, 17
27:35
28:8, 15

SELECTED REFERENCES TO PRAYER IN THE EPISTLES
ROMANS

1:8–10
8:15, 26–27, 34
9:1–5
10:1–2, 13
11:33–36
12:12

COLOSSIANS
1:2–3, 9–12
4:2–3, 12

I THESSALONIANS
1:2–3
2:13
3:9–13
5:23, 25

2 THESSALONIANS
1:2–3, 11–12
2:13, 16–17
3:1–2, 5, 16, 18

I TIMOTHY
1:2, 12–14, 17
2:1–2, 8
4:4–5
5:5

2 TIMOTHY
1:2–4, 16, 18
4:18, 22

TITUS
1:4

PHILEMON
3–6, 22

HEBREWS
2:17–18
4:13–16

SELECTED REFERENCES TO PRAYER IN REVELATION
1:4–6
4:8–11
5:8–14
6:9–11, 16 17
7:9–12
8:3–4
11:16–17
15:3–4
16:5–7
19:1–6
22:17, 20, 21

SELECTED REFERENCES ABOUT WORSHIP IN SCRIPTURE
VERSES THAT GIVE INSIGHT INTO TRUE WORSHIP
Genesis 22:1–19
Exodus 3:1–6; 20:1–18; 25:22; 34
Deuteronomy 26:5–11
Joshua 5:13–15
1 Chronicles 29:10–22
Job 1:20–21
Psalm 5:7; 27:4; 29:2; 45:11; 47:1–2; 66:1–4; 86:8–10; 95:6–7; 96:1–13; 99; 1:1–5; 132:1–7; 138:2
Isaiah 6; 66:1–2, 22–24
Ezekiel 1:28–3:27
Matthew 2:10–11; 4:10; 14:33; 15:25; 28:9, 16–17
Mark 14:3–9
Luke 10:38–42
John 2:13–17; 4:23–24; 9:35–38; 11:32; 12:1–8
Philippians 3:3
Hebrews 12:28–29
Revelation 14:6–7

VERSES THAT GIVE INSIGHT ON SACRIFICES THAT BELIEVERS
CAN OFFER TO GOD

Psalm 51:16–17; 141:2
Micah 6:6–8
Romans 12:1–2; 15:16
Philippians 4:18
Hebrews 13:15–16
1 Peter 2:5
Revelation 5:8; 8:3–4

VERSES THAT GIVE INSIGHT INTO UNACCEPTABLE WORSHIP

Exodus 32; 34:14
Leviticus 10:1–11
Deuteronomy 4:15–24
1 Samuel 13:8–14
2 Samuel 6:1–9
Job 31:24–28
Isaiah 2:6–11; 48:11
Amos 5:21–27
Malachi 1:6–14, 3:13–15
Mark 7:6–7

VERSES THAT GIVE REASONS TO PRAISE GOD

Psalms 9:11–12; 63:3; 66:20; 68:19; 98:1–3; 103:1–5; 113;
        119:164, 171; 139:17–18; 147; 148:5–6, 13; 149:4
Daniel 4:34–37
Romans 11:33–36; 16:25–27
2 Corinthians 1:3–5
Ephesians 1:3; 3:20–21
1 Peter 1:3
Jude 24–25
Revelation 4:8–11; 5:9–10; 7:10; 11:15–18; 15:3–4; 16:5, 7;
        19:1–8

VERSES THAT GIVE REASONS TO THANK GOD

Psalms 7:17; 18:49–50; 118:1, 21, 28–29;
139:14–16
Acts 27:35
Romans 1:8
1 Corinthians 1:4–7
2 Corinthians 2:14; 4:15; 8:16; 9:12, 15
Philippians 1:3
Colossians 1:3; 3:17
1 Thessalonians 2:13; 5:18
1 Timothy 1:12–14

Appendix 2:
Ideas to
Stimulate Prayer

1. Ask God to give you and your spiritual leadership the "grace" of prayer (the motivation and enablement to pray). Remember that true prayer is a work of God as He brings a person to understand his complete helplessness apart from Christ. If we forget this principle, the following suggestions will only produce works of the flesh.

2. Link prayer as a part of all of life and ministry. For example, let prayer be a vital part of all your responsibilities—committee work, counseling, planning, leadership meetings. Exercise your faith before you exercise your will.

3. Possible suggestions for worship services:

   a. Pray for your pastor before and during the worship service.

   b. Seek to give people an opportunity to be prayed over after the service.

   c. Consider having prayer teams to have the ministry of prayer during the worship service.

246

4. Have special prayer emphasis weeks to give training in prayer and special opportunities to gather for prayer.

5. Encourage the formation of prayer groups that form to pray for common prayer burdens.

6. Encourage prayer partnerships so that everyone has some prayer support.

7. Consider organizing prayer retreats and days of fasting.

8. Give vision for pastoral prayer support team:

   a. 7 people—one day a week assigned to each one

   b. 31 people—one day a month assigned to each person

9. Consider forming prayer-visitation teams by which you reach out to believers and unbelievers and offer to pray for them. One way to do this is to approach people and simply ask how you can pray for them. Call or visit them again to see how God is answering your prayer. Apply this to neighbors, coworkers, clients, and other acquaintances. Ask God to lead you to people who are open to learn of the true and living God.

10. Continually listen to God for His plans.

Notes

CHAPTER 4
Turning Your Temptations into Victorious Prayer

1. Wesley Duewel, *Measure Your Life: 17 Ways to Evaluate Your Life from God's Perspective* (Grand Rapids: Zondervan, 1992), 107–8.

CHAPTER 5
Experiencing the Spirit's Motivation in Prayer

1. Francis McGaw, *Praying Hyde* (Minneapolis: Bethany Fellowship, 1979), 49.
2. The "accuser of our brethren" is one of the names of Satan and is found in Revelation 12:10.

CHAPTER 6
Receiving Strength to Believe God

1. Richard Harvey, *Seventy Years of Miracles* (Camp Hill, Pa.: Horizon House, 1998), 64–65.
2. Ibid., 66.

CHAPTER 7
Being Guided in Prayer

1. Wesley Duewel, *Touch the World Through Prayer* (Grand Rapids: Zondervan, 1986), 61–62.
2. NPNN e-mail, 6 Sept 2001.
3. Bill Thrasher, *Living the Life God Has Planned: A Guide to Knowing God's Will* (Chicago: Moody, 2001), 21–22.

CHAPTER 11
Learning George Mueller's Secret

1. A. T. Pierson, *George Mueller of Bristol* (New York: F. H. Revell, 1905), 73.
2. Ibid., 43.
3. Ibid., 49.
4. Doug McIntosh, *God Up Close* (Chicago: Moody, 1998), 112.

CHAPTER 12
Experiencing True Prosperity

1. For an example of this truth in respect to Romans 12:1–2, see pages 129–30 of my book *Living the Life God Has Planned* (Chicago: Moody, 2001).
2. As you pray the commands of Scripture, you can pray with the absolute assurance that they are God's will. You can also pray with the assurance that God will give you the motivation and enablement to obey them.

CHAPTER 14
Learning to Pray Scripture

1. See appendix I for a list of other scriptural prayers.

CHAPTER 15
Realizing the Struggle of Prayer

1. Don Currin, "The Barrenness of a Busy Life," *The Awakener*, Fall 2000, Vol. 8, No. 2. Used by permission.
2. Quoted in *Luis Palau Responds*, Vol. 15, 2000.
3. Dr. J. Sidlow Baxter, from a message preached at Bibleland Conference, Boca Raton, Fla. Date unknown.

CHAPTER 17
Gaining Strength Through Prayer

1. Steve Farrar, *Point Man* (Portland, Oreg.: Multnomah, 1990), 154–55.
2. Richard Foster, *Celebration of Discipline* (San Francisco: Harper and Row, 1978), 31.

CHAPTER 18
Realizing God's Desire to Bless You

1. Don Currin, "The Barrenness of a Busy Life," *The Awakener*, Fall 2000, Vol. 8, No. 2. Used by permission.

CHAPTER 20
Learning When to Fast

1. Philip Schaff, *History of the Christian Church*, Vol. 2 (Grand Rapids, Eerdmans, 1973), 377.
2. Richard Foster, *Celebration of Discipline* (San Francisco: Harper San Francisco, 1988), 51.

CHAPTER 21
Experiencing the Benefits of Fasting

1. Bob Moeller, "Smog in the Sanctuary," *Leadership Magazine*, Fall 1994, 79–80. Excerpted from *Love in Action: Dealing with Conflict in Your Church* (Sisters, Oreg.: Multnomah, 1994). Used by permission of the author.
2. Entire books have been written on the physical benefits of fasting. See Herbert Shelton, *Fasting Can Save Your Life* (Bridgeport, Conn.: Natural Hygiene Press, 1978).
3. John Piper, *A Hunger for God: Desiring God Through Fasting and Prayer* (Wheaton, Ill.: Crossway, 1997), 93.
4. Bill Bright, *The Coming Revival: America's Call to Fast, Pray and Seek God's Face* (Orlando: New Life Publications, 1995), 94–95. The list is my arrangement of his material.
5. Richard Foster, *Celebration of Discipline* (San Francisco: Harper San Francisco, 1988), 56.

CHAPTER 22
Getting Started

1. Joel 2:15–16 is an example of a congregational fast. You can find examples of calls to a national fast in Judah in 2 Chronicles 20:3. (For a helpful pamphlet on conducting a congregational fast, International Awakening Ministry of Wheaton, Illinois, publishes "The Solemn Assembly.")
2. Judges 20:26–28 and Acts 13:3 are two scriptural illustrations of guidance given during times of fasting. For a more complete study of seeking God's will, see my book *Living the Life God Has Planned* (Chicago: Moody, 2001).
3. The story of Pastor Henson's prayer, told in chapter 21, shows the purpose of fasting for God's deliverance and protection (cf. 2 Chronicles 20:3–4, Ezra 8:21–23, Esther 4:16).

CHAPTER 25
Transforming Your Anxiety into Peace

1. J. C. Ryle, *Christian Leaders of the 18th Century* (Carlisle, Pa.: Banner of Truth Trust, 1981), 83.
2. Ibid., 84.

CHAPTER 26
Knowing When to Keep Praying

1. I am indebted to T. W. Hunt's insights from his teaching on this passage.

CHAPTER 27
Experiencing the Goodness of Praise

1. C. S. Lewis, *Reflections on the Psalms* (New York: Harcourt, Brace, Jovanovich, 1958), 93.
2. Ronald Allen and Gordon Borror, *Worship: Rediscovering the Missing Jewel* (Portland, Oreg.: Multnomah, 1982), 29.

CHAPTER 28
Understanding the Meaning of True Worship

1. Story told by I. M. Anderson, *Moody Monthly,* February 1926.
2. Quoted by Steve and Valerie Bell, *Made to Be Loved: Enjoying Intimacy with God and Your Spouse* (Chicago: Moody, 1999), 150.

CHAPTER 29
Abiding in the Lord

1. Hannah Whitall Smith, *The Christian's Secret of a Happy Life* (Old Tappan, N.J.: Fleming H. Revell, 1952), 46–47.
2. For a look of how to develop the practice of meditation on Scripture see my book *Living the Life God Has Planned* (Chicago: Moody, 2001), 162–67.

CHAPTER 30
Cultivating a Lifestyle of Worship

1. A. W. Tozer, *Whatever Happened to Worship* (Camp Hill, Pa: Christian Publications, 1985), 56.

More from Bill Thrasher and Moody Publishers

Believing God for His Best

A personal story that will walk you through the author's journey through singleness, and toward marriage. The anecdotal style, coupled with godly wisdom, will inspire singles to trust God for His very best.

ISBN: 0-8024-5573-5

Living the Life God Has Planned

ISBN: 0-8024-3699-4

When we come to know God's wondrous attributes and His flawless character, we can set about living the life He intended. In this rich and bountiful book, Bill Thrasher unveils the key to living in the center of God's will. By focusing on God's character, we are aligned with His will. When we learn to abide in Him, to take all of our needs and frustrations to Him, everything falls into place.

A JOURNEY TO VICTORIOUS PRAYING TEAM

ACQUIRING EDITOR:
Greg Thornton

COPY EDITOR:
Cheryl Dunlop

BACK COVER COPY:
Julie Allyson-Ieron, Joy Media

COVER DESIGN:
Ragont Design

INTERIOR DESIGN:
Ragont Design

PRINTING AND BINDING:
Versa Press Incorporated

The typeface for the text of this book is
Centaur MT